Cops, Crooks, Courts & Spooks

Also by Ray Clift and published by Ginninderra Press

Fiction

The Journey of Hamlyn Baylis Wells
Always In Denial
Smithy's Cupboard
Shaken & Stirred
Shalom Samuel
The Last Journey of Hamlin Baylis Wells
She Walks the Line

Non-fiction

Maybe Blue Ghosts
It's a Fine Line

Ray Clift

Cops, Crooks, Courts & Spooks

Acknowledgements

To family and friends.
Especially to Ann, and my daughters Kerry and Jo.
To my writers' group, Sharon Kernot and her partner Gary MacRae in particular, who assisted me all the way.
To Ashley Lance from SA Police, who laboriously accessed police archives.
To publishers past and present, especially Ginninderra Press, who put me on the map.
And finally to GE, who placed the words in my brain through automatic writing.

Cops, Crooks, Courts & Spooks
ISBN 978 1 74027 902 4
Copyright © Ray Clift 2015

First published in this form 2015 by
GINNINDERRA PRESS
PO Box 3461 Port Adelaide 5015
www.ginninderrapress.com.au

Contents

Introduction   7

Prologue   9

Part I   11

Part II   79

Part III   141

Author's Note

I am seventy-six years young. That statistic means different things for different people. For me, just reaching three score and sixteen years is a milestone. Time for me to set my affairs in order, as they say, and tie up loose ends while my memory still remains. The stories told here are about real and surreal happenings I have experienced. I use GE and Me when I take down his words but sometimes when I'm walking he comes straight out with material which I record as just Q and A. Some names have been changed to protect the integrity and privacy of those involved. However, GE remains my constant companion until I meet him later on in that other world – much later on, I hope, because life is too full at the moment. I have many things to do. Like paint the house, plaster the cracks and fix a few things. Normal stuff really. Don't get me wrong, reader. Just because I appear to be talking to my inner man, then that's cool with me. You see, I am well and truly grounded.

Introduction

I'm not everybody's standard copybook cop, though friends and family surmise that I have played the part as well as other comrades. Most of them know of my nuances and my penchant for things beyond the veil. After all, there are paperbacks dotted all over the house with much New Age material, so it was no surprise to them when I started speaking to a spiritual guide named Grey Eagle who was named from the start GE, although he insisted on using my full Christian name of Raymond.

I enjoyed my thirty-two years as a South Australian police officer and later on the fifteen years working as a court sheriff's officer. They all contributed to the crucible of memories which was a boon once I started to write. There were chats with GE on walks, there were dreams and automatic writing, which became a feature of my life for many years. Much of the advice from GE is humorous but I suspect he won't suffer a fool and I sense at times his exasperation when I ask for too much, because the pages fill up with gibberish, crossed lines and at times Celtic-like designs with many loops and whorls. Those images signal the time for me to stop and let it rest for a while.

GE cleared a path for some of my writings to be published. Publication is not the simplest world to break into – it is like trying to crack a thimble with a toothpick. I am profoundly grateful for his help. He has most recently helped with the construction of this book. It took some conversations with him to get it right. Like the following.

GE: Do your early life and the police and so on first. Put us in the middle and, finally, more cop stories about some of your mates and their take on the job.

Me: OK.

The session concluded, as always, with a 'God bless'.

Once the words came out, I felt his joy coming through with the familiar smell of his buffalo-hide cape, which was always draped across his shoulders in defiance of all weathers. I never asked him if he felt the cold. A bit stupid, really, because they are without the sensations that we as humans feel. He related our times together as Red Indians in the nineteenth century. His silence, once it gathered storm, was gold at times and, once written, was enough for me to know he liked the story. Yet I had doubts about what an editor would think and asked GE.

GE: Let the Universe work it out. Stop worrying.

Me: What about a title?

GE: You figure it out.

I had a restless few nights with all sorts of wild images of what the title would be. Thus ended the discussion.

Prologue

The young man was horizontal on a mechanic's crawl board. He was engaged in drilling through the underside of a semi-trailer. On the top of the semi-trailer was a mate: Geoff 'Sluggo' Bull, waiting for the drill bit to emerge. Both the young men had served mechanical apprenticeships with the South Australian Tramway and Busway Trust and both were in good spirits on that morning in the late 1950s. Unbeknown to both, the extension lead for the drill was not earthed. Unbeknown to both, the handyman had emptied the firm's teapot over the two-pin plug.

The young man was instantly and violently electrocuted as the 240-volt surge suddenly hit him. He felt intense pain, shock and convulsions; he went into something similar to a cardiac arrest. He was gripped tightly by the current and did not know what was happening. He felt himself slowly moving towards a bright light and along a green tunnel. The speed of movement accelerated to a rush and at the end of the tunnel was a bright white flashing light. People were walking about carrying children and animals in their arms but they were dressed in modern clothes, so this was not another time in another era. He was not aware of any voices he knew but clearly heard some voices saying, 'Go back. There is much to do. You will remember this in time and write about it.' Distantly, yet with clarity, he was pushed backwards and ambled away from the lights. In his thoughts, he guessed he was probably dying. An outing to a drive-in theatre had been organised for the evening and he clearly remembered thinking, well, I won't make it there tonight.

The rush back commenced when Geoff, alert now, heard the noise below and looked down and saw the man's predicament. He acted with great presence of mind, kicking the power source off and dragging the young man out. It took a while to do so because his friend was still unconscious.

The man was out for over six minutes. He saw his inert body lying on a stretcher and watched the people staring with solemn looks. A sheet was put over his face just as he entered his body. He shook himself and stood up. He saw the boss was finishing a peanut bar with bits and pieces dripping from his mouth.

As was the tough style of uncomplaining people in those days, he was sent home by taxi; he had no medical treatment and resumed work the next day and then resigned. Geoff had saved his life. And it would not be forgotten.

The near-death experience of the young man was the third one in his life. He was seven years of age, suffering from a chest infection, when his first occurred (though some say it was an out of body experience, or OBE). At home in his bed, he felt a spiralling, spinning vibration. His heart missed a beat – a long beat. He was thrust along a tunnel, at the end of which was a strange bright light. Some people told him to go back, which he did.

Until the age of twelve, there was not one night that he didn't encounter OBEs which caused him to float out of his body around his home. He would come back from the ceiling and wake up in the morning exhausted. His mother was alarmed at this when he spoke to her, and her response was to seek medical treatment. The doctor's conclusion was 'It's just his imagination.' No treatment or explanations were given for his experiences and it was a decade before he read some books on the subject.

His journey began in earnest after he was married and other married friends started to speak about their fears as well. But concrete proof was still needed.

Part I

'In a time of universal deceit, telling the truth is a revolutionary act.' –
George Orwell

1

Childhood

I grew up in South Payneham, a suburb of Adelaide. I was born a Lang. Two years later I was a Clift, in the nurturing arms of Henry and Ivy Clift, a couple who had scrimped and saved throughout the Depression, labouring, gold panning and gardening. Ivy ironed and cooked, taking on the chores of a tough generation who had inherited the fine soils of the Adelaide plains. They were sure their child would receive as much education, as much comfort, as could be mustered in those tight years. And I did. Associated always with their love of family were their strong conscience and their help to others less fortunate, though they were nearly on the poverty line themselves. Many times I watched Dad hand over money to people even poorer than them.

My maternal grandfather lived in an old van which some would describe as a humpy. Situated some distance from our house, it was a ramshackle abode, humble and modest, under the shade of a giant loquat tree. My grandfather was nicknamed Turp, a name which had been given to him after a bad night on the turps. He was an alcoholic for much of his life, a fact which I gleaned from family snippets. The wheel of life for him had been stuck at the bottom and it is not hard to guess why. He was a victim of the Depression. Sometimes he spoke of it in whispers, sometimes he almost shouted from the rooftops, depending on the amount of grog consumed during his recall. The hopelessness of those times turned many to the grog, which must have been, for a short time, a dulled release.

In between his bouts of the horrors, I saw glimpses of a fine man. A man with a great knowledge of native plants and birds, a greenie to a certain degree, well before that term was hatched. I can attest to his recycling habits and the end-product of those habits. Each morning at the same time he would loose an endless stream of urine onto the base of the loquat tree, which bore continuous fruit, delicious fruit, almost tennis ball size. That tree would have been justified in loving Turp, its best patron.

'He wasn't always like that, Raymond,' my mum said, using my full name as she always did when she wished to make a point. She would add, 'His drunkenness just grew.'

He was a man of habit, the best being when he would emerge dressed for work – bike clips in place and with his old woollen but clean flannel underwear, short sleeves, regardless of the cold, his old grey fedora hat clamped tightly on his head – and pedal furiously out onto the road. He was bound for the Greenhill quarries, where he worked as a powder monkey. Turp was highly respected by his employers for his work ethic and he never sneaked grog while at work.

It was always dusk when he returned, riding his bike without lights, covertly ducking the circling cops always trying to catch him. Drunkenness was his usual breach of the law but they never were able to catch him on his trip. He would lob in his abode, take a few swigs of his wine and then Mum would serve him his favourite meal: two boiled eggs and toast. Out of view of all except me, the burgeoning know-all, he would consume in great gasping swallows, with a stop for breath, at least half a flagon of his favourite stash, Congo – an impertinent brew, Dad always said. If he was not asleep after his meal, I would return and listen attentively while he regaled me with tales of the bush. At the same time I would roll endlessly his favourite makings – two ounces of Capstan rubbed fine-cut tobacco – and all smoked with the air of an aristocrat sweeping his arms about with great flourish; he would always end the chapter with dramatic gestures.

His experiences became a shared experience, insofar as I learned tolerance of many people, good or bad. It served me well throughout my life and encapsulated forever in my mind an understanding of how addictions can form, like a dark shadow possessing us from time to time. We keep it under control most of our lives, under lock and key. Some find that key in times of stress and the shadow flies out, bent on a path of destruction.

The country was, because of its roots, very much a racist domain, though many of those citizens would not accept that judgement, and probably still don't. For instance, the prime minister told the American army chiefs that he did not want to see African American soldiers on our shores: we were a white Anglo-Saxon Protestant community. Disparaging remarks could be heard about the Irish, the Catholics and any other groups that did not fit the mould. Nothing was said about the Aborigines that I can remember. And in our little provincial world, still clinging to Mother England, we prospered reasonably – as far as rations would allow, that is. The women went to work in the jobs men vacated to enter the armed forces. My mother did not join up. Nor did Dad. He was in munitions before the war but, try as he might, he was not released for army duties. This rankled with him as another man up the street received some white feathers in the mail, but Dad did not say much about that thoughtless gesture.

He grew potatoes in rubber tyres, and gathered up manure in his barrow. Much livestock roamed in paddocks back then. He was six foot two and thin as a rake, stooped later, and, despite being thin, extremely strong. He cycled thirty miles each day to his place of employment and worked a forty-eight-hour week, as everyone did. On Sundays he would cycle six miles to his second job as a gardener at Tusmore. I never once heard him complain. Later on, I used to ride with him.

Mum knitted all day, and at night in the winter they would sit by an open stove cracking their almond shells, saving the kernels for sale and using the shells as a fuel source. And of course, they listened to the old valve radio.

I was eight years old, visiting relatives at Magill, in the foothills of Adelaide, on a warm October day many years ago. My two cousins and I were playing outside in the dry creek bed which flowed through that area, flooding in winter. A magic place to be: tadpoles, wild fennel, pebbles of all hues and nearby red gums with their overhanging branches to swing from. Many games could be played. Time was forgotten. A truck chassis acted as a bridge. The day passed by swiftly. We were called inside. Time to go home, back to Payneham.

The gas producer had to be fired up. Petrol was rationed. Wartime restrictions were in place. My face was grubby and my grubbiness would soon have consequences. It was important for children in those days to present to the world a scrubbed face, even if in that scrubbing some layers of skin were removed. We dreaded what followed. The flannel, named for its texture, the cure-all face washer, was produced and we were all lined up. Depending on your skill, or your experience, you were first in line. I was on the end of the line. The grubby flannel was passed on from parent to parent and from each child's face the bacteria were also passed on, so I was the last in line to receive them. Generally the cloth would contain residue spittle, mucus, possibly blood or any other secretions.

Mum's strong hand held my head still, the other with the flannel making circular motions and then up and down. I was reacting like a gum leaf turning on edge to avoid the full impact of the sun, at the same time Mum telling me to hold still.

Unable to stand it any more, I broke free yelling out, 'Pooh, someone's wiped their bum on this.'

A hush fell on all present. The oldest female relative and the one who claimed ownership of the flannel (if it had been me, I would have shut up) now enraged, red in the face, eyes blazing and glasses fogging up, looked at me and said, 'You should keep him in line. He's around adults too much.'

But at least he was not around adults who kept flannels with old skid marks on them. I was quickly ushered outside and we mounted the old Essex Super Six without side curtains and drove home at the incredible pace of twenty miles per hour. Mum smirked all the way.

Dad remarked, 'Her hygiene was always suspect, Ivy.'

I sat in the back with wind cooling my red, scrubbed face and blowing away the smell of that flannel.

It was some time before we saw them again.

All of the children in the street played outside until 9 p.m., usually games of Japanese versus Aussies. The Aussies always won. The seventeen- to eighteen-year-olds who fought in New Guinea were conscripted and quickly grew into men. The giant war Hoover sucked them up and deposited them in the wild jungles with only broom handles to hold, instead of guns, for a short time. Their heroism saved our country.

There were American soldiers camped opposite on the school oval. Mum said, 'Like tailors' dummies.' They were kind to us kids and the old folks, so they were popular with us.

Gypsies were also camped opposite. I played with their children. Their mother once said, 'You know things,' but I didn't get it then; now of course I know exactly what she saw in me. The police later moved them on because some old nosey neighbour made a complaint. I missed the smell of her cooking with garlic which, permeated with the smell of tomatoes, flooded the air.

On hot days we put out a blanket on the lawn and, I guess now, spiders just crawled over us in the night. The ice man called each day and the street kids picked up the shreds of ice and sucked on them.

Out in the street on a sunny day in 1943, a man was running fast up our street wearing khaki trousers and a shirt. No hat. It was an uncle, a man I did not like. His green army shirt dripped with sweat; his black protruding eyes were wide open. He did not glance in my direction when he ran into our drive. A green Chevrolet army utility was close by. It stopped outside our house. Two soldiers stepped out, wearing armbands with 'MP' emblazoned in red and black; they were big men, brutal-looking and angry, and they carried wooden clubs, about four feet long. Mum came out. They brushed past her. We watched as they dragged out the uncle. Blood was streaming down his face and I saw that the clubs were saturated in blood. One of the MPs was tapping him on the head with a club. Not a word was spoken outside. No attempt to stem the flow of blood was made. The uncle looked white and pale and his eyes were closed. They tied his hands behind him. Then both of the MPs picked him up and threw him bodily a distance of about six feet. I heard his head crack as he hit the cabin. He lay there motionless. They lit up cigarettes and giggled to each other for a few minutes then, without a word, got in their vehicle and drove off.

Later that night, Dad told Mum that the uncle was a deserter. He added that the MPs had been brutal. I agreed – silently.

Later on, I was reading the back page of the *Adelaide Truth*. That was taboo for me, as it was considered to be a scandal rag. I was about to read the last paragraph on an army deserter who had received twelve lashes for something I had not known of, carnal something or other, when the paper was abruptly snatched from my grasp. I was then consigned to the Possum pages, which did not have much drama in them. The lashed person was of course the uncle.

I possessed a great memory for faces and some years later, when in the police, I saw one of the club wielders in the cells at the Adelaide watch house. I fingerprinted him and read his papers. His record showed that during the war he had been dishonourably discharged from the army for assault. The hypocrisy of the man who so brutally dealt with the uncle flooded into my thoughts.

I grew up with parents who were really closet socialists. It is no wonder I inherited that ethic, though after the war Dad voted for the conservatives, who lifted the rationing of many goods – Labor, just like in England, was kicked out of office for a while. I picked up the stray dogs, shared toys with others and always protected the underdogs at school, and all of those deeds were coupled with a mouth that occasionally spoke out of turn, particularly at school. I soon, and rapidly, learned that speaking out wasn't much fun. It would get one the cane, and frequently; so the truth got masked in order to cope with the social constraints. That at least taught me the value of self-discipline. Once they thought they had broken you, you complied. It was like a run-through to the armed forces at a later date.

My last infringement which resulted in a caning was when one poor girl standing in line, like awaiting the guillotine, suddenly pooed herself. The teacher struck out with a cane, striking the debris, which instantly spattered his face. I laughed until I cried and the resulting caning was severe. He caned me with one hand, the other hand still wiping the mess from his face. I recovered, whether intentionally or by accident.

I had a loose bowel then and broke wind a lot. Dad always ordered, 'Get outside and shake yourself.' I would comply and at the time wondered what good that would do. Chubby Checker introduced the Twist around then and I mused whether he got started by a father sending him outside.

Like all grotty kids, we used to laugh when someone farted in class and it was murder holding our tongues when the teacher went around staring in our faces and saying with dribble on his lips, 'Did you just fart?' It was worth the cane just to break the ice and admit to it. I still remember it when I was belted. 'Oh God, stop.'

Tears and laughter reverberated in the classroom. We were really quite a tough lot. Some of the kids' fathers were killed in the war and some mothers just ran away and left their children to the grandparents, or to the

Salvos. That was no picnic because I schooled with a couple of kids who ended in the boys' homes.

Mick, a mate, lived with his granny and used to pinch money out of her purse until his dad came home from the war with one leg and belted the hell out of his son. Mick's mother ran away with a US soldier and we heard later that she jumped in front of a train when she found out that the soldier was married. A very sad tale.

2

Adolescence

It was time to seek employment. Looking back, I wonder where I would be now if I had taken on what my father advised – industrial chemistry. I chose a trade, not realising I would be better suited to a people-friendly style. I chose the trade because it was not a sissy job, and besides, all men then worked on their own cars and were self-sufficient people.

My apprenticeship was at the Municipal Tramway Trust – the bus and tram organisation which ran Adelaide's public transport. The place made everything from the ground up: it was really an amazing adventure. All races mixed without any problems: Poles, Germans, Greeks, Serbs, all together. I still have a fondness for those groups, particularly the Poles. Wiser now, I do not think it was a waste of five years, because I give much credit to the Tramway Trust for its character building. The several other apprentices were similar in background but most of them would not have known the poverty or unusual circumstances that I grew up in.

We were like lambs to the slaughter with those tradesmen. Those who controlled us were tough men, all excellent tradesmen, nearly all war veterans and some having fought on the opposite side. The practical jokes played on us young ones had to be seen to be believed. It was a learning curve and one had to toughen up quickly, before the job and at school.

I attended the local technical high school and passed with flying colours in all subjects but maths. I studied reasonably hard and, apart from a few self-generated outbursts, I succeeded in that institution. I loved sports but was no great shakes at it until I played lacrosse. I left high school having qualified and continued playing lacrosse. I played for East Torrens and practised on the Norwood oval and finally made the state trials. I copped a blow to the head with a stick and was knocked out in that game and subsequently on at least three other occasions. The concussions were severe and so I took up weight training. It seemed to be a safer option than nursing concussion on Sundays and having stitches to the head on a few occasions. I trained at various gyms and soon got involved with that fraternity. The buzz acquired in gaining much muscle and strength appealed to me as a seventeen-year-old.

An eventual Mr Australia, a gentle giant named Tom Lardner, was a great guy who coached us all. No sign of drugs back then, just sheer hard work. By age eighteen, I was pressing 200 pounds above my head. Not clean and jerking – just by sheer willpower, pressing the weight. It was easy, if jerking it, to make the bar another eighty pounds heavier.

In order to provide extra strength and muscle, we all consumed a large amount of protein; the choice was skim milk. That beverage has some unsocial side effects: not being quickly digested, it makes the consumer fart. A gym full of grunting males all farting, and not in unison, is, depending on the listener's sense of humour or disgust, a chorus, an almost tuneful one at that. Visually, it was even funnier. Imagine a weightlifter lying prone on a bench. He attempts a bench press far above his maximum. Two mates are on each end of the bar, ready to guide the weight either back to the rack or try to help him reach his goal. His eyes are bulging; the blood is flowing through his arms and pectorals. He has already taken in a full breath and on the hard part, the upward thrust, he reaches a sticking point and trying to gain another breath takes a short gasp, puffing it slowly out, like a woman giving birth. Almost at the pinnacle, the undigested skim milk, now no longer able to be contained, lets out a warning squeak followed by a huge fart. The gym erupts in laughter. The two catchers are barely able to carry out their function, distracted from their task. The poor grunting man, now stuck with the giant weight, midway between his chest and the rack, cannot stop it slowly dropping to his chest. He is now farting, staccato. It's serious and some control is gained by others, who move the weight off his chest. He jumps off the bench and chases the two catchers. He is an accomplished wrestler and they stay out of his way till closing time. Two days later, they are friends again.

We had to curtail our skim milk consumption. It was ruining our social lives, dancing in particular, and the band always seemed to stop when you let one go. The band always masked the noise but I do remember that a crowd of us were spoken to by a bouncer. One of my friends, a good Catholic from the west end of the city, farted in church, just on entry when he bent down. His mother cracked him across the skull with her shoe. Dad tried for years to stop my farting and made me eat outside for a time. He was a man of impeccable manners and could not stand breaking wind.

Early in our employment we were subjected to ridicule, like being send to the store to obtain false objects such as a left-handed hammer, a bottle of sparks and a bubble for a spirit level, to name a few. We dreaded the lunch orders, which we were sent out to obtain from a nearby delicatessen. We would blurt out the orders. Dotted in amongst them would be items such as honey turnover and lettuce, a pregnant tart and a bottle of pickled foreskins. The ladies in the shop were all mature women and they would give a sympathetic look and either shake their heads or send back a caustic note with the lunch orders.

One had to grow up quickly. At that point we started, rather sadly, to lose the innocence of children. There were the initiation ceremonies which involved actual indecent assault. We would be held down, trousers removed and all of our pubic area smeared with heavy grease. Very hard to remove. Later on, I got my own back when, in the police, I arrested one of the initiators, the ringleader, for a drink-driving matter.

I noted that in all of those initiation ceremonies not one of the so-called wog immigrants participated. I guess they had seen enough of intimidation in their lives.

I recall some of the folk. Big Jack was a giant Russian who had survived the war and the Soviets and escaped. In his good-humoured way he told me in broken English how he had worked on the Snowy River scheme and finally settled in Adelaide. Smelling of his secret vodka stash, he had a favourite story. 'Cheeky Boy,' he said (he would always call me Cheeky Boy), 'I find rat that is dead,' and he would kick the body of a dead rat; rats were plentiful in the big shed then. 'Rat is eighteen years old,' he said, then with a quizzical look on his face he would start laughing out loud and say, 'You know how I know is eighteen years old?'

I would shrug and laugh along with him, then for the punchline he would blurt out between giggles, 'He has birth certificate up arse.'

I do not know how many times I heard this joke, which was really an obituary to a dead rat and is still funny after all these years.

I had not developed the dexterity or the coordination required to handle some of the tasks at work. Very early in my apprenticeship, I was detailed to assist an elderly tradesman to service a double-decker bus which was over a pit in the MTT depot. It was my task, on the signal from the tradesman in the pit below, to pour oil into the fluid flywheel, and the tradesman would check the level while in the pit. Being a lover of music, I thought the tradesman looked just like Ray Bolger, the dancer who had played the Tin Man in the Judy Garland movie *The Wizard of Oz* – he was encased in a tin outfit throughout the movie, which I had recently seen. The tradesman would not be expecting that he would soon be drenched in oil while in the pit. As well, when he shrieked out loud, 'Jesus Christ,' muffled by the outpouring of oil, I dropped the funnel and it fell and plopped straight on the his head. It was a cold day. I sneezed, and in doing so lost control of the oil can totally. The oil, which had a certain type of viscosity, had tumbled without warning on the Ray Bolger lookalike's head and he shrieked in shock and spluttered with the double dose of oil which soaked his head. The funnel was a perfect fit to his pointed head, which was not unlike the Tin Man's. The enraged man emerged from the pit, like a submarine emerging from the sea, the funnel still attached to his head. He was shouting and advancing rapidly towards me. I suppressed a giggle, thinking that he really did look like the Tin Man. He was not able to see where I was, due to the oil which had saturated his head, blinding his vision. The duty St John man cleaned him up and allowed him to go home.

I was a lad to be watched from that point in my career, though most of the tradesmen wanted a blow-by-blow description of the incident. It caused much amusement and I felt that if I didn't make it as a tradesman I'd make it as a comedian.

The Mad Man was a wild-looking fellow with long hair flowing to his shoulders. He would regularly dip his hair into the bucket of tempering oil in the blacksmith's shop, claiming that it made his hair lush. He also operated a huge steam hammer. He would crack walnuts with it, such was his skill. He had a certificate from the then Parkside Mental Hospital declaring him to be sane. He had it displayed and proudly told any readers of the certificate that he could produce evidence of his sanity but the rest of us could not, which was true, I suppose.

The foreman of the blacksmith shop had St Vitus' Dance. Most of us did not know what that was. He kept it hidden. When his hand started to shake, he would place it in his dust jacket pocket. He was due to instruct me on how to use the buff polisher-grinder attached to a grindstone. Just before that, a tradesman who I thought was being kind but was actually setting me up showed me how to use the buff. He demonstrated that I should pick up the article and shake it with my hand continuously. While I was doing this, along came the poor afflicted foreman. He came over and stopped my hand shaking. He glared at me and strode off. I later saw his hand when it was on the move again. I instantly got the message. It was a cruel joke to play on the poor old bloke and I am sure that he never forgave me. I stayed out of his way for a long time.

The arc welding tent abutted the Botanic Gardens. During the night, possums would have a feast on leftover lunches. A new welder started work. He was an instant expert on everything, particularly squirrels. One of the old Italians heard him bragging about squirrels and set him up. We guessed the expert had never seen a possum, which was correct. The expert was told that a squirrel was in the next tent; perhaps he could feed it. Angry male possums in the wild do not take kindly to human intervention, as the expert found out. He bent down and held out his hand, which the enraged possum promptly bit. It then ran up his arm and scratched his face, badly. The expert ran shrieking from the tent with the possum still attached to his ear and blood running down his face. I am sad to record that I laughed. I was joined by the entire shop.

One of the tradesmen spent most of his days berating his wife because she had, in his words, 'gone frigid'. He would talk to anyone in earshot about it. One day he came to work rubbing his hands in glee and told all in attendance that his wife was about to be served with a notice called 'Restoration of Conjugal Rights', which was apparently on the books then,. Whether other men resorted to this drastic form of manipulation I do not know, but the tradesman could hardly contain himself until knock-off time. He was not at work for about a week and when he turned up looking dejected, one of the men asked about the notice. He was told that when he arrived home he had found the place empty. His wife had cleared out with the next-door neighbour, leaving the official notice on the only table left, with a note. The official notice had a suspect brown smelly streak on it. The note said that Fred, the former neighbour, didn't need a notice to have sex with her.

I was by 1954 well into weight training and had some boxing lessons from an older apprentice who was, incidentally, an accredited boxer. Having toughened up, I determined not to merely accept backhanded slaps from some of the older tradesmen. One tried to belt me over the back of the head. He was also partially intoxicated, due to his stash of cheap wine secreted under the work bench. When he swung his hand towards me, I ducked, grabbed him by the overalls collar and slammed him up against the wall, completely taking the wind out of his sails.

From then on, and forever after, I would never ever be a punching bag to any other prospective bully. Les, the big genial Hungarian ex-boxing champ, gave me a big hug and said he saw it coming. No one, of course, was foolish enough to tackle Les as he was not only a champion boxer, but also an immensely strong man.

Towards the end of my five years at the tramways, I worked with a violent, indeed mad, Croatian. He was feared by his own countrymen. He was also a conceited man. He would not allow any apprentice to carry out mechanical repairs. We could not understand this attitude because he was, in fact, not a good mechanic. He was instructed to remove the worm wheel inside a differential on a bus which was over a pit. In order to remove that part of the differential, one unscrews the bolts around the outside perimeter of the differential casing and, before removing the worm wheel, the axles have to be removed. This is necessary as the axles pass through the middle of the housing which holds the worm wheel in place. Simple stuff, I thought.

I started to undo the axle bolts while the violent man was in the pit. He shouted to me to stop. I asked him what he was doing. I then saw, to my horror, that with a huge jemmy bar he was levering the worm wheel, still held fast by the axles.

I yelled at him to stop. 'F—ing wait till I undo the axles.'

He swore at me so I just stood up and waited for the result. It wasn't long in coming – a loud crack which echoed across the workshop, announcing that he had cracked the differential housings – and immediately brought the foreman running. As I was telling the foreman what happened, out of the pit emerged the now enraged mechanic. He ran towards me with the jemmy bar raised over his head. I retreated, and then ran as fast as I could with big C in pursuit taking swipes at the air with the giant jemmy bar. The foreman and others joined in the chase, eventually running him down. He was restrained, foaming at the mouth, eyes wide and staring, shouting out swear words. He was taken away by an ambulance and the police. We never saw him again and we were told he had been carrying false papers.

That was about as close as I could recall to a near-death experience without the apparitions usually attached, such as tunnels and departed folk telling one to go back. I reckon I heard a spirit voice say, 'Run, Ray, as fast as you can.' I obeyed as fast as I could.

I received a first-class pass in my trade exams, but the job bored me. A smart boss figured it out at the end of my apprenticeship, and I was out. A bit of a shock actually. I went through a few jobs. Before the end of my apprenticeship I was called up for National Service and commenced six months' training in the RAN at *Cerberus* in Victoria followed by three months at sea on the Royal Australian Navy's flagship HMAS *Sydney*, an aircraft carrier.

3

At Sea

I heard a loud bang. We had hit an old mine near the boilers – dangerous stuff. The chief stoker told us to stay calm, just in case there was an explosion – not exactly what we wanted to hear. His advice was that if it reached the point where the boilers burst, it was goodnight for all of us. But it worked out and the mine was a dud.

I was a young sailor at sea. Being on a carrier was a buzz. I did not find the training overly difficult. We were all self-disciplined people from birth. The food was good and one got to meet interesting people. Our ship was named after an illustrious forebear. The Royal Navy in the 1940s named her HMS *Terrible* but the RAN renamed her *Sydney III*. She had twin steam turbine engines, and oil-fired boilers were used to propel the turbines. The stokers and the officers, both commissioned and non-commissioned, worked amid the sweaty 120-degree heat and the ear-splitting noise of engines and other ancillary equipment.

Once again, though, we hit a mine.

Because of the intense heat of the boilers, a pressure entrance door was always closed for fear of flashback. Flashback was when a stream of fire could shoot out of the boiler, burning everyone in the near vicinity. Great care was taken to avoid this. I and my shipmates were told of the hazards. There was some apprehensiveness among us and probably within the minds of the regular staff, as they were sealed in the engine room along with us.

The ship was steaming through twenty- to thirty-foot swells in the Southern Ocean, a notorious ocean for massive waves. One day in 1956, an emergency drill exercise was called. The ship started to slow down. Looking at the faces, the strained looks on the regular staff's faces, I could see this was more than a drill. The chief stoker gathered all the youngest members about him and said as quietly as possible that it appeared the ship had bumped another old German World War I mine. There were still some of them floating about, and it was not known if this one was active. We had been told that the chief had been on HMAS *Perth* when she was sunk in the Sundra Straits by the Japanese in the 1940s. By a sheer miracle he had made it out of the engine room to the sea; he was captured by the enemy and miraculously survived the horrific Japanese POW camps. He returned to Australia and remained in the navy. To the sailors, he was not a hero; he was a survivor.

The young men listened intently to what he had to say. They were all gazing at the eighty or more steps up out of the engine room. He told them to forget about it. If the mine exploded, we were done for. He went on to say that if a bulkhead was breached, then the oncoming water would boil. Once it did that, a better and faster death would be to swallow as much sea water as possible, thus quickly drowning. I had experienced this in my youth. I determined that it would be better to die then and there.

The exercise was called off after divers checked the mine and found it inactive. I felt personally that there was some guidance that prevented me panicking. Later in life, my suspicions were confirmed when I chatted with GE, my guide.

While in the RAN, I saw sea duties in the Southern Ocean, seeing whales and icebergs, and also in north Queensland's waters. Quite a startling contrast. However, I felt that if I had taken up the RAN's offer, I might have ended up a hopeless drunk, so I returned to civilian life.

During those formative years, I maintained what has been a lifelong interest in weight resistance training. Without any drugs and starting young, my bones and frame grew to allow me an entry into the South Australian Fire Brigade and the SA Police.

My time in the fire brigade was short-lived as the police force beckoned, but I still recall the buzz of jumping into a net from two storeys; riding on the back of the open Leyland unit heading to a fire; sliding down the pole. Great adventure for a young man. However, I didn't much enjoy being 200 feet up a ladder while it was swivelled around. But it is all in the training, and the brigade taught us not to fear heights, just to respect them. I still do, in spite of having fallen off ladders many times.

4

Early Days in the Police

The Thebarton police barracks housed the mounted division, the traffic division, workshops and administration. It was where I began my training. The training and discipline were what I expected. The RAN had been a good starting point. Personal study was required, but I did not find it difficult. Apart from a hiccup early in the piece and a correction on my part, and with the instructor's support, I passed, ranking second, and after a graduation parade was released on the unsuspecting public.

I clearly remember a controversial arrest early in my career. One evening, Sergeant Gunner and I arrived at the scene of an accident involving a motorcyclist and a car at the east end of Rundle Street. The injured rider was groaning in pain on the roadway. He had a broken thigh and his leg was twisted at an angle. The car driver was bending over him and talking. He was wearing the robes of a Catholic priest. Just from his demeanour and the strong smell of grog, I could tell he was more than moderately drunk. Besides, he had his hat off fanning the poor bloke's face, which I thought was a trifle unusual. Blowing in a bag was only done then if one had a hot pie. It was arrest back then: note the demeanour of the driver, give him a one-way ride to the station and then an examination by a doctor.

I quickly drew a plan of the scene while Gunner was talking to the driver in the back of the police car. Gunner quietly told me we might have some trouble with this arrest when back at the station. Meanwhile, the chap was having a bit of a snore in the back. The cop shop was close by and when we woke him, he headed to the toilet. Refreshed, he was guided to the charging window and then locked up for a short time. He had made some admissions to Gunner.

After an initial plea of guilty, he changed it and we were later required in court; it was a packed courtroom. I saw the Commissioner in the back row. I was called and sworn in. His lawyer went for my jugular as soon as I was asked how affected by liquor he had been. I said 'Moderately' and in recall I believed I was being kind to him with that assessment.

The lawyer thought he was on a winner and I watched him as he metaphorically tap-danced while framing a question. Then with a triumphant smirk he called out in a loud voice, 'And what do you, a man of tender years, attribute your wealth of experience to, to come up with that assessment?' He probably thought I had been a cadet, a cop since school.

I masked my smirk, thinking, I've got you now, dickhead. I turned and looked at the old, wise senior magistrate (SM), who allowed me to speak about my experience. And I gave him a ball-by-ball account of Turp, of the many drunks I had seen with him, about the drunken uncle, the RAN and other blokes. I was only halfway through when the lawyer, not now tap-dancing, tried to stop me. I continued, ignoring him.

The SM asked me what my granddad's name was. I enlightened him.

He said, 'Turp – Turp Smith. How is he now?' and we then carried on an informal chat about how Mum tried to get him off the grog.

The SM said, 'Sad case. A great powder monkey and when sober a good man. Yes, yes, thank you, constable.' He then said to the broken lawyer, 'Anything else you want to ask, Mr H? No questions?'

I left the court smiling and I could see the Commissioner was also smiling. The driver was convicted. He appealed and lost, and was in the mire with his seniors.

May in 1959 was a stormy time: thunder, lightning, rain, foggy nights. Not a good time to be out. I was with Thomson at 2 a.m. on St Bernard's Road in Magill, driving the police vehicle. There was not much happening on the radio network. On nights like that, when we were not responding to jobs, one looked for work. We tried hard; nothing was about.

Then an agitated middle-aged woman flagged us down in her car. This could lead to something, was my initial reaction. She quickly told us in a shaky Polish accent that something was floating about in the nearby St George's cemetery. She drove away out of the cold. I had some experience with the supernatural but Thomson, a macho lad, much loved by the female gender, was not too keen to take it any further. I must say that the prospect did not exactly appeal to me but we had to do something.

I said, 'Relax. It's a good night to visit a graveyard, and besides, some of my relations are interred there.'

Thomson nodded, much quieter than usual.

Thunder again; lightning flashed. Thomson was walking in my footsteps. If I stopped, he stopped. He was almost stapled to me. Our breathing was loud and fast. Slowly we crept, like in a scene from a Martin and Lewis movie. The radio went off and we both jumped and then turned it off. I saw a big yellow dog further ahead, sitting on its haunches. It looked up in the sky and howled mournfully, baying like a wolf, and by then the hairs were right up on the back of my neck as we inched towards the hound from hell. Its tail was down. Its hairs were raised on the back of his neck. We were all in a state.

We shuffled around. Our shoes were getting soaked in the mud. We saw an enclosure covered in old ivy. The rusty gate was slightly ajar and it squeaked as I pushed it open. I shone the police torch around and the beam, being of poor quality, finally came to rest on a black shape. A vampire, perhaps, was my first guess. We approached and, on pulling back the black cowl on the shape, discovered a rather attractive girl under the cowl. Thomson suddenly came to life, exclaiming that we must check her out.

We lifted her to her feet and realised she was in a trance. Removing her from the scary place, we went outside. And the dog was overjoyed. His former demeanour was gone and he was racing up and jumping over her. But she was still out and we half-carried her back to the car. The dog came too, happy to be out of that place of death.

A woman police officer, Prue, arrived. She also felt the creeps when we related the story to her.

A doctor examined the girl. She was sane, not involved with the black arts. By then, there were rumours racing through the town about such matters. She had through her own endeavours attempted to engage with the departed but an empty graveyard at night is not the way to go. We took her home and informed her parents. Nowadays, I would have reacted differently.

Probationary Constable R.J. Clift was then posted to the city watch house and beat duties and car patrols, the car patrols extending across the Adelaide suburbs. Shift work was an essential part of the job. The inspector in charge of my watch was an imposing, intelligent, wise man and a humorist who treated his staff fairly and with care. My sergeant was Douglas Wylie Nation, a great bloke, inside and outside the job. I felt very fortunate.

Apart from foot patrols and occasional car patrols, also included were some traffic control, jury guards, prisoner escorts, court orderly duties and guarding sick prisoners being moved from institutions to hospital. Coming from a restricted background, I disregarded the fact that the pay was dismal. I just loved the variety. I thrived on it. It was a consummation to be enjoyed. Why then were the old constables bending our ears saying, 'The job's fucked'? I thought at the time, grumbling old buggers, why don't they just get on with it? How would they like to do what I had done for the last five years? It's very true: one cannot put an old head on young shoulders and expect them to know it all.

Police parades at the start of the day's duties were military fashion. We lined up in three ranks, right dressed. Roll call duties were read out, and correspondence collected. It was almost like a graduation parade: once forward, march out, receive correspondence, salute and return to ranks. Then a fall-out to duties, receiving equipment and so forth.

An older constable from the traffic division was with us for a while, having committed some minor infraction. He was a giant bloke nicknamed 'Hoofer'. When Hoofer's name was called out, he stepped backwards, not forwards, and plonked his equally giant foot in a nearby trash can. He quickly realised he could not get his foot out in the time required, and then an amazingly funny thing occurred. He marched out, took his correspondence, saluted and about turn marched back, all the time with the trash can on his giant foot. It broke up the parade. It broke up our dear boss Ted. He gave us two minutes to get the grins off our faces. That was a magic moment.

I observed that many people I worked with disliked the beat. With my background, I accepted it, and realised my expectations were not all that high. To be fair, many of them were cadets, joining at sixteen, longing for CIB – supposedly more exciting work. At that stage, I was just happy to follow, just enjoy. I found out that was not encouraged. One was expected to move on, accept more responsibility.

Night shift on foot patrol was a rather exciting time for me. I arrested a man for kicking a street sign down. He took off and by the time I caught him, he was ready for a fight. I took the first blow and then knocked him down. I dragged him to a call box – no portables back then – and while I was phoning for assistance he pushed my head into the call box. By the time I extracted my head, with my large ears being somewhat of an impediment, I went searching for him. I found him hiding, grabbed him and frogmarched him to the city watch house, where he pleaded guilty. I did not charge him with assault seeing as in the process of arresting him I got the second hit in. The boss laughed when I told him.

After countless arrests on night shift, waiting around from knock-off until court at 10 a.m., I began to have some sympathy for the older officers. The older ones certainly shied away from arrests on night shift; some of them, if they thought their arrests were going to plead guilty, would get their mates to cover for them in court. That had some very bad stings in the tail, particularly if you got called into the witness box giving your mate's name instead of yours. Some got away with it for years.

One night I walked the beat with a real old gent who all the young ones thought was stupid. He turned out to be highly intelligent, somewhat erratic and definitely intransigent. He ducked away when we were in the closed Central Markets area, where many homeless people slept. He then emerged wearing a bear suit and proceeded to run around the market scaring the tripe out of the drunks, having a good time. Then he would ride a police bike round the streets wearing his bear suit. Many reports from the public came in about a very hairy man with a police hat riding a bike without lights. When he retired, the reports stopped.

Occasionally, the old guys would open up and you realised how much was stored in their brains. They knew every crook in the state. Though they never bragged about it, most of the old guys were heroes, having taken guns, knives, axes and broken bottles off people, all with a minimum of fuss. Many of them retired as court staff, never having reached high ranks. I was learning fast: never volunteer information, particularly in court, and confine yourself to yes or no, I don't know, can't recall.

I was involved in one of many high-speed chases in our FJ Holdens.

No seat belts, no heaters, no air conditioning and no indicators. One chase around the Torrens Lake area ended with us in the lake. Funny at the time.

Auto accidents were not funny. Hopelessly watching people burn to death in a car is decidedly not funny. Telling relatives the news is also not funny.

There always seemed to be a sudden death on each shift. I had to admit to the city morgue a man who had drowned in a vat of Shiraz in the Barossa Valley. The coroner's chest-cutter licked his finger, wiped the body with it and remarked what a good vintage it was. That was funny.

The city morgue was then located in the West Terrace cemetery, quite a fun place to be. I suppose the architects chose this location, something akin to horses for courses – sort of keep the dead, buried and unburied, together; this suited the tidy Victorian-age mentality. It was a nondescript red-brick building with no signs saying this was the way to the morgue, particularly one-way signs. 'You are now standing near the morgue, please speak in whispers.' Inside, the unburied awaiting their earthly remains' final destination were accommodated in the sixteen fridges or, in times of overcrowding, on slabs inside.

The north-west city patrol was designated to admit bodies from other areas. I seemed to be on this patrol a lot more than others, so you either toughened up or tried to swap. It doesn't take long to develop a morbid gallows sense of humour; most hospital orderlies, morgue attendants and undertakers have it.

Dreadful jokes were played on new chums. The best was when a new chum was driving into the area. Any others still admitting bodies would turn off the lights, hush voices and wait. One of us would hold a hand over the light switch when the new boy was reaching in the dark for the light. We would grab his hand. Imagine how much fun that was. Another was, if there was an empty fridge, one of us would get inside with a sheet on. You can guess what happened when the door was opened and the comic genius sprang to life.

The story about to be related was, however, not a trick. Someone, probably a necrophiliac, kept breaking into the morgue and disarraying the bodies. A night-shift guard was put on duty. You can guess that the youngest, most innocent-looking kid was detailed, under protest of course. He was driven to the morgue with instructions to ring the city watch house on the hour. He did so, I should imagine fearfully. At about 4 a.m. he fell asleep. He was awakened later by a naked corpse standing over him coughing, still with the tag on his toe.

The corpse turned out to be an old World War II prisoner of war who was in a catatonic state when certified. He was still alive and, nonplussed, picked up the phone, stated who he was and that he wanted out of there, and then said, 'By the way, the young cop has shot through.'

The officer had fled screaming. We never heard from him again. As an unusual incident, it created great amusement to us cruel cops. The young fellow was not amused.

I was in the Supreme Court seated at the dock in the public gallery when I saw the old senior sergeant court officer nodding off to sleep. He was snoring and must have woken up because of a noise. He jumped to his feet and, pointing a long bony, nicotine-stained finger at the public gallery, called out in a loud voice, which was cracking with rage, 'Stop farting.' The accusing finger traversed the entire gallery, like a bee waiting to land. A deadly hush fell over the courtroom. The officials were quiet. The judge sat up. No one spoke as the witch-finder looked left to right. Finally the judge, mercifully breaking the ice, bowed and left the court. The now-shocked senior sergeant, realising that he might have been the mystery wind-breaker, sat down. I bet the judge and his staff had a real cackle outside.

There was an anti-larrikin squad, which I thought was a strange name to give a squad. Australian larrikins won two world wars. Part of the essential character of Australia was the larrikin. Larrikins organised the Eureka Stockade. But, with their sexual innuendoes bandied about by a press looking for something juicy to write about, bodgies and widgies shocked the Adelaide Christian community, though the bodgies and widgies of those days would seem like choir boys and girls nowadays. Once the initial clean-up of the bodgie and widgie 'menace' was over, the squad was maintained as it should be, to collate intelligence on real crime, to control street behaviour by plain thugs and other criminals. I volunteered to do a tour of three to six months after the menace, many of whose members I knew, were dispersed. Lots of experience was gained in working with the oldies of the squad, many of them close to seven foot tall, as opposed to my five foot eleven and a half.

On a Sunday night in Hindley Street, a night I will never forget, I was involved in a severe incident. An armed criminal, wanted in Canada for murder, had abducted a boy at gunpoint, forcing him into a stolen car. At a set of traffic lights, the boy jumped out and advised police. Kevin was driving the police car, Dave was in the passenger seat and I was in the rear right seat. The vehicle number of the stolen car was broadcast, and it was there in front of us. Kevin drove alongside. The criminal looked, and then reached into his jacket. Kevin rammed the car into the kerb. The crim started reversing away with the mudguard of the police car attached. I jumped out and reached for the driver's door. He was reaching for his gun and reversing at the same time. Dave caught up. We chased the vehicle on foot to West Terrace, where the criminal drove straight towards me in reverse. Regulations at this time permitted an officer, if his life was in danger, with no other way of apprehending a felon, to fire his gun. We both fired, peppering the windscreen but missing him. He turned off and drove away, very fast, turning left into Currie Street. In his wrecked police car, Kev caught up to him, slamming him again into the kerb. By the time Dave and I caught up, Kevin had the crim by the throat.

The charge of attempted murder wouldn't stick. It was broken down to illegal use. He received two years and was eventually deported back to Canada. Kevin received an honourable mention. No one spoke to Dave or me about it. We were in limbo until the magistrate stated that the shooting was justified. No counselling, just a few beers.

I vowed never to draw a police weapon again. As a result, one inspector told me that I could be arrested for impersonating a police officer. I replied, 'Better than impersonating a human being.' He was as thick as two planks. Probably didn't get it until I had transferred. I stayed out of his way. Poor Kevin died later on down the track, far too young.

Patrol cars covered the area of Norwood, a large suburban complex outside of the city with a court attached. The local police staff carried out mobile duties on a motorcycle outfit. The duties were enquiries, follow-ups, serving summonses, attending domestics or any one of a myriad of other tasks. The office duties were taken in turns and some court work – processing of prisoners, care of prisoners and much paperwork, such as court fines, registrations and driver tests – rounded off duties. It was generally a very busy place. One Sunday afternoon, I broke the record of typing twenty-eight accident reports; all accidents were reported then, irrespective of damage. Also, if patrols were too busy, we were first on the scene to any job, minor or serious, that came up, and there was no radio contact. We performed traffic control on weeknights from 4 to 6 p.m. without a break at the busy intersection of North Terrace and Hackney Road. That's just for starters. On night shift, one officer walked the Norwood Parade on beat from 11 p.m. until 3 a.m., then swapping over. A pretty boring beat with nothing much happening.

We were tasked to serve a traffic summons in the market garden area east of Adelaide. I was the rider of a 650cc Tiger Triumph motorcycle and sidecar. Seated in the sidecar was Constable D. Constable D had to make a stop at the Payneham police station; he was suffering from mild diarrhoea. We forged on and entered the driveway of the expansive property where the owner and possible driver named in the summons resided. The place seemed deserted. No answer was received in spite of our loud policemen's knock. We roamed around the back of the property. It seemed obvious that no one was home. I was parked near what was actually a chicken coop. I thought that possibly someone might have been in the back. D and I looked around and I saw a room with a green door, but it was locked. Time to go.

Suddenly, in the term used then, D. was 'caught short'. I could see he was not going any further. He was unbuckling his trousers, squatting. Not wishing to remain in his view and he not wishing to stay in mine, I went outside, feeling a bit apprehensive at his decision to evacuate his bowels in the chook house. But his need was immediate and necessity is the mother of invention. The sight of a policeman in full uniform, still wearing his hat and about to perform his ablutions, has remained with me since then.

What happened next was something to be witnessed. The mother of the property, an old lady in an Italian widow's outfit, suddenly emerged from behind the green door. Her eyes lit upon the squatting police officer, still with his hat on. Instantly enraged at the sight, she rushed towards him. I, at that stage, had heard the commotion, and walking quickly into the chook house I saw the old lady, now shrieking like a banshee in Italian, flaying into the now standing officer with a piece of what I would say was wormwood.

The officer fled and jumped in the sidecar and yelled, 'Get going.'

I would have, but the bike would not start. By this time, the old banshee was flaying both of us with stems of agapanthus that were growing nearby. We and the bike were covered with the agapanthus, of which she seemed to have an inexhaustible supply. As we finally made our getaway, I looked back at her and she seemed to be like a miniature statue of liberty, swishing the air with more of her plentiful supply of agapanthus.

I went back later that day with a shovel, served the summons, buried the watery substance and had a hilarious hour laughing with the owner of the property with his Italian-speaking mother.

I would occasionally see the man in the street and he would laugh and say, 'Hey, Ray, Mama wants you to come back and we can laugh at that all over again.'

Sadly she died before I had time to go back.

As for D, he was left safely ensconced at his place of abode to recover from his malady and to reflect on his unfortunate choice of toilet selection. He had to remain at his home on sick leave for two consecutive days. I had two choices with regard to the flower-covered Triumph motorcycle: either secretly clean it, and make no mention of the incident, or tell all of my colleagues. I chose the latter and had them all in fits of laughter, as one can imagine. Yes, I did clean up the motorcycle too.

Senior Sergeant John Alfred Charles Broad would have to be one of the most colourful characters I ever met. A remarkable man of some genius, I suspect, about six feet four, with handsome almost Errol Flynn looks but twice his size. I remember him with great fondness. His style, which is hard to emulate, may never be repeated. Tough when he wanted to be, compassionate in his deeds – not his words – he had high moral principles, was a non-drinker and an egalitarian, and he had the presence and movement of an athlete. He expected the best of his staff, didn't praise much, and didn't criticise much. A look was enough from him. He dispensed justice rather than law and his style promoted self-discipline. He had a focus on what was right, irrespective of whether the lines of the law were blurred. There was a slight bit of a control freak in him.

He bred champion bantams. Many a prisoner in the morning demanded his bantam eggs for breakfast. I know because there was a drunk sleeping it off in the cells on one busy night shift. I had supposedly locked the cell door, when at 6 a.m. I was greeted in the front office by the prisoner, who requested I tell Jack to get eggs for breakfast. This would normally be a court martial offence. I locked him back inside the cell. Jack was not a man to be lied to. When I told him, he laughed loud but did nothing else. Just his departing look told me to be more careful next time.

He told me some time later he disliked officers who picked on drunks to get a score up. Jack, if he could, would withdraw charges the next day, as he was also the prosecutor for the district.

It was also required for the officer to administer punishment as directed by the court. When a kid was brought in shaking, he would make a deal. He would bang on the desk. The child was to yell out in a loud voice, with one proviso: if the kid told others, he would go to his house and see that his father administered punishment. I never knew of a kid that broke his rules.

Jack had pet names for all of us. Because of my crew cut (frowned on then) and my pointed head, he always called me 'Bullet Head'.

We had a few gang problems on the Norwood Parade. Jack called me one day to take him to the Parade on the motorcycle outfit. He was too big to sit in the sidecar – he used to balance precariously like a gorilla sitting on a toolbox. As we were crawling up the Parade, the leader of a nearby pack called out a disparaging remark. And promptly Jack called him over, told him to take his hat off and swatted him on the head, like a fly, with the motorcycle gauntlet. This dill fell on the roadway. Jack told me to leave him. Back at the station I told my partner about it. Rex showed me the glove: there were two big ball bearings in it. 'Don't mess with Jack.'

With wife-bashers, his technique, though it was highly illegal and would get him the sack now, was very simple. Round the fellow up, take him into the empty courtroom, leave him waiting. Jack would enter with a rolled-up newspaper, being very kind. He would talk about how men should be men, and not hit women. He would move behind the fellow and then like a flash belt him over the head with the *Advertiser*. If you were hit by Jack, you would stay down. He was cool all the time and then, to the copper who was witnessing, he would say something so that he would later, if needed, testify that nothing happened.

'Bullet Head, go up to Carter's Bakery and get three buttered buns.'
Which I did.

One felon said, 'I don't like butter.'

To which Jack replied, 'Listen, boofhead, you're like a greyhound: all balls and elbows. You'll eat it.'

The felon ate it later. Then Jack would walk up to the felon's house, sit down and talk to the battered wife. A cuppa and a buttered bun. Not much paperwork in that. They sure were different times.

The Hon. Don Dunstan, member for Norwood, no lover of police, spoke in the House of Assembly about Jack in glowing terms. However, none of us could come up to his style and get away with it. The danger in copying him was the possibility of being charged with assault, which was then, as it is now, a criminal offence.

An elderly man died while masturbating with a ring spanner. When we were eventually about to take him to the morgue, his wife asked us if she could have the spanner back. Property must remain on a body until all medical evidence is completed but then we were able to return the spanner to her intact. Whether she left it on the mantelpiece, we don't know.

5

Traffic

In 1962, after my marriage to Marlene, the mother of my two delightful daughters, Kerry and Joanne, I sought a transfer to permanent day shift. There was one available in Adelaide traffic control. When I took it, some of my police friends were surprised, as traffic control was considered a dead-end job. I found the environment rewarding and enjoyed it. Besides, I could do more weight training, and being in the city all day was just like being a beat cop except one was home in the evenings. I didn't regret the tapestry of traffic control. It may have put my career on a temporary hold, but living life was more important to me. The buzz of directing traffic control has never left me and never will. I would still be able to direct traffic at the busiest intersection that could be thrown at me. Great mates were there yet try standing on a 100-degree day for three hours waving arms. Underpants creep upwards but 'Can't scratch your behind,' I was told. Must be dignified. But dignity disappears when a jock itch starts.

Mick G was a colourful character, a laconic ex-Australian Army policeman, who never said much. Mick G was also the Hollywood actor Robert Ryan lookalike on the phone book cover for years. In spite of his size, he could move like a ballet dancer. He was a joy to watch on traffic control. I made the mistake of going out with him on a day of grog. After his twenty pints, and my eight, he put me in a cab and sent me home. Before I got too inebriated, Mick told me he had been an assistant executioner of the Japanese war criminals on Moratai. I asked him how he felt about it and in his nonchalant style he told me it was justice for his mates who died in POW camps.

One dark rainy night two weeks later, I was hit by a driver at North

Terrace and King William Street. I was able to jump on the bonnet and hang on until the terrified female driver stopped. When she stopped, her windscreen wipers, which I was holding onto, came off in my hands. She sent a bill to SAPOL for the wipers. It was ignored of course.

I was detailed on one occasion to perform traffic control at the intersection of Rundle Street and Gawler Place, before Rundle Mall was created. There was bumper-to-bumper traffic each way and we were sharing a half-hour about on the point. The off point man also stood on the sidelines assisting in pedestrian control. On that particular day, big Mick G., the Robert Ryan lookalike, was on pedestrian control. I turned to the west, presented my right hand in a stopping motion and was quite shocked at what I saw. Not five metres away was a man on a bicycle, standing up and pedalling furiously, intending to go against my signal. The shock was that the man on the bicycle was completely naked. He whizzed into the intersection and Mick grabbed him off his bike. The naked wriggling man was held in a firm grip, with the bike careering off to the left. Mick had the squirming man held fast in his iron grip and, being a well known identity, was responding to passing motorists with a friendly wave. In order to carry out the manoeuvre – and I have never seen this before or since – Mick transferred the naked bloke onto his hip and in that way was able to wave as well. It was similar to the movement that mothers carry out when holding their child and carrying out the myriad of tasks mothers are expected to do. While in this position, the wriggling man realised he was not going to get free.

At that time, the elegant ladies who worked at the big general stores were flocking back after their lunch break. One of these elegant ladies, with a bejewelled finger, pearls perched on her neck over the top of a black blouse, and with Helena Rubinstein badge firmly attached, ran over to Mick. She looked straight in the naked man's face and said, quite loudly, 'You should be ashamed of yourself. What would your mother think?' That statement from a dignified, middle-aged lady, and spoken with some clarity, was a perfect choice of words. The squirming man stopped and then buried his head into the giant shoulders of his restrainer. More surprising for me was that, in spite of this cold day, his genitals were still moving in the breeze, somewhat languidly, but nevertheless moving.

A patrol car soon arrived and its driver arrested the man, who was now very embarrassed at the ever-growing crowd of spectators, all having a look at the strangest of strange situations. Shortly before the arrival of his one-way taxi to the city watch house, he was covered up with an old blanket, provided by another elegant lady from Myers cosmetics. I believe he was admitted to the then Hillcrest Hospital, and I heard of no more of his fate.

At the time I was on traffic control, the term 'whistle-blower' had only a literal meaning. We were issued with a whistle in order to control traffic. I was on point duty at the Hindmarsh roundabout at the Port Road and Park Terrace intersection. This was before traffic lights. In order to maintain a proper flow, right turns had to be banned and four signs had been placed on the roundabout to assist the traffic flow. I was, at the time, in company with a new traffic man who was known for his love of the whistle. He was in the centre directing traffic. At the time, he had a heavy cold; I detected an odour possibly of port wine on his breath.

Drivers were constantly disobeying the signals. It was not long before he had a huge congestion of cars backed up and it was soon chaos. Our whistle-blower inserted the whistle in his mouth, coughing and blowing the instrument at the same time. No one would have had a clue what his intentions were. By the time I had run over to take control, he was lying on his back like a beetle with legs in the air, blowing the whistle and coughing at the same time in frustration. The whole situation seemed surreal. I helped him to his feet and tried to rescue the whistle, but he held fast to it like a child with a dummy. He ran over to the side of the road, fell down onto the footpath and recommenced his one-man band. Luckily the pointless tune was soon stopped by a passing patrol car; the police bundled him into the back and drove off. He still had his whistle in his mouth. I noted that the officers had wound down their windows to diminish the sound of the pointless one-note tune.

The whistle-blower was soon out of the job. At that time, there was sadly no going-away show, no presentation of a whistle. His bacteria-loaded whistle had been consigned to a dustbin.

My next posting was to Thebarton as an accident enquiries officer. It was more a follow-up, tie-up-loose-ends task, which resulted in many court appearances on behalf of the prosecution unit.

The sergeant at Burnside, when my next posting came about, was Bill.

An outback northern South Australian chap whose experience in those jurisdictions was enormous, he had much Aboriginal folklore under his belt due to frequent patrols of the lands. Respected by the elders, he enjoyed his time there. I felt he was wasted on a suburban station, but he was nearing the end of his career and I guess his thoughts were on retirement, and justly so given all the community service he had provided.

Another one of those laconic outback cops who did the job as fairly and impartially as time would permit, Bill said that the first job in policing the Aborigines was to sit down with the elders to determine some parameters and some concessions, and then be true to your word after that meeting. I have met a lot of indigenous folk since then. None would speak ill of Bill.

During this time and from 1964 I was a member of Emergency Ops Group (EOG). This was a forerunner of the full-time Star Force. It

---

POLICE HEADQUARTERS
ADELAIDE
SOUTH AUSTRALIA

TELEPHONE: 217 0333
BOX No. 1539, G.P.O,
ADELAIDE, 5001

OUR REF.

YOUR REF.

For inclusion in Personal File

SGT. 1/C CLIFT, E.
REGION 'D' TRAFFIC

The Emergency Operations Group ceased as a "call-out" group on the 30th June, 1979, following the formation of the Special Tasks and Rescue Force. A number of former E.O.G. members with rescue/recovery expertise are now members of the Special Tasks and Rescue Force and the Logistics Support Unit.

Emergency Operations Group units have been responsible for many rescue and recovery operations over the years, many of which have been extremely dangerous. Personnel have carried out these duties in a manner which has reflected credit on themselves and the Police Department. It is also to the credit of E.O.G. operators that serious accidents have been kept to an absolute minimum. One serious accident has occurred in E.O.G. operations extending over 20 years.

Your contribution to the excellent services performed by the Emergency Operations Group will be noted in your personal file.

21/1/80   Deputy Commissioner of Police was largely a volunteer, seconded group, which carried out cliff rescues, missing person rescues and some sea exercises with the aqualung squad.

I remained on EOG until 1970 and then was posted, having passed the sergeant's exam, to G Patrols in Adelaide. There, I was on a team as one of the senior constables and was a mentor to newly graduated constables. Most of them pulled up quickly. Many became high-ranking officers. Some are still in the force.

In 1970 I was detailed as an arrest team member on the huge Vietnam Moratorium demonstration at the intersection of King William Street and North Terrace. A huge crowd jammed the intersection. They were given an order by Assistant Commissioner Ted, an articulate, tough but fair boss, who was an immaculate-looking man. (Ted received a blast of some substance in his face and became blind in one eye. He stayed in the job until retirement age.)

The crowd wouldn't budge. The tactic for removal was simple: one sergeant and three men would approach a front line, instructing the person to move on and leave. Many did. Those who didn't were arrested, removed to a van, photographed, placed in the back and taken to the city watch house. The violent ones – there were some – were overcome and handcuffed. I arrested fifteen demonstrators that day.

While holding a defendant at the van, there was an incident. An old digger, I assumed, dressed in civvies and wearing an RSL badge, jumped out of the crowd, punched a protester in the stomach and disappeared. Despite the protests from the defendant, I still put him into the back of the van. Later in court, he squawked to the magistrate. The magistrate asked me what I had seen and I told him that it had happened, but I wasn't about to release the defendant to catch the digger. He asked me if I had tried very hard. I replied no, not really. I agreed with the Vietnam commitment and our soldiers needed all the support they could muster.

Just before the protest was totally dispersed, I was standing near the Parliament building with a superintendent, and some spittle was coming down from a window. An MP was spitting on the cops below. She didn't have the guts to join the demonstration, but wanted to get her dollar's worth. I never voted for her again.

The Royal Commission headed by Justice Bright was a new experience for me. I gave evidence as to what I had heard, seen and done. I asked a few questions that begged an answer and walked out wondering what a waste of time, energy and money it was.

I was rostered on the Labor Day weekend, a public holiday, to work with a junior man, Alistair, and we responded to a job at Jolly's boat house on the Torrens Lake, where pedal boats were hired out. The river banks were covered with people enjoying the sunshine. The manager pointed out to me a man who had hired one of his boats for the day. The man refused to return to the shore. I saw that the man had placed a large tree trunk on the pedal boat. I asked the manager something like 'What do you want us to do about it?' And did he have, say, a dinghy with an outboard that we could use? No! As usual, expect the twenty-four-hour social-worker coppers to fix it.

I spotted a rowing eight going past. I called them into the bank, jumped in and demanded they follow the boat. Which they did. Boarding was a problem. When we got close enough, the jerk in the pedal boat moved away. I leaped from the rowing eight, luckily managing to reach the pedal boat, but with wet feet. The rowing eight boys retrieved my hat. By that time I was really pissed off. I let him know about it by a belt over the back of his head. While he was holding his head, I grabbed the tiller and headed in to shore. The crowds on the bank were having a hell of a time watching history being made. We reached the shore. I had, meantime, ditched the tree trunk.

There was more bad news. The jerk didn't speak English; he was on leave from a ship in Port Adelaide. I weighed it up, thought about the paperwork, emptied out his pockets. The manager said he owed $16. That was promptly plunked in the manager's hands; he was happy. I sent the jerk off and that was that!

Operations enquired, 'What was the result of the Torrens Lake episode?'

I replied, 'Civil action – money handed over. Nothing further.'

Next day, of course, Alistair opened up his gob. I was asked the next day by Communications if I had caught any fish.

We received a call to attend a country bus service depot. The driver had shut the door after returning from the Yorke Peninsula with a bus load of Aboriginal folks. A white bloke in the back claimed he had been robbed. I enquired if he had been drinking, gone to sleep and ended up with an empty wallet. Pretty hard to retrieve it but I thought I would try. I addressed all the folks, looked around and saw a few I knew. I told them that I would check and if there were any warrants out I would make some arrests. I made a deal. I would walk out the bus and come back in five minutes expecting to see the money on the floor of the bus.

When I went back in, it was there. I let the bus go and the jerk was counting his money. He said $10 was missing. I said, 'Think yourself lucky. Get going that way, but not on the bus.'

Two days later I responded in the boss's office to a complaint from the bus guy over $10. After I had told him the story, he said, 'Cliffy, you've been kissed by a Chinaman.'

I was out on patrol with Al in Hindmarsh when we received a call from an old lady who had had rocks thrown at her roof for the last two weeks. The neighbours wanted to buy her house. She refused, so they harassed her. I found out the neighbours were home so I gathered all the rocks and knocked on the door. A Turkish-looking bloke opened the door and stuck his nose out – big mistake. I grabbed it, hauled him out and chucked all the rocks back into his house. He was strongly advised to limit his rock throwing. No more trouble there, but I did advise Al of the folly of emulating some of my tactics. The days of instant justice were nearly over.

Les Lee and I attended the sudden death of a poor lad who had swallowed a corrosive poison. He died in agony. He was from a family of high achievers; he was the odd man out. His body was taken to the Queen Elizabeth Hospital for autopsy and identification. The body was on a gurney with a sheet covering. The arrangements were that I would stand in the ID room behind the glass. A relative would identify the body.

Les called out, 'Ready.'

I pressed the curtain button and at the same time withdrew the sheet covering the body. The entire family had gathered: mum, dad, uncles, aunts, cousins and probably people from the street. They had a look of horror on their faces.

I looked down and saw the poor lad's tongue lolling out and his eyes open. In the process of trying to get his tongue back and close his eyes with one hand, I was also trying to close the curtain by pressing the switch. The switch started the curtain opening and closing, the tongue still lolled out and the eyes were still open, and all the relatives craned forward, craned back, with the movement of the opening and shutting of the blasted curtain.

Meanwhile, a band of interns and nurses were watching and having their own brand of fun, all laughing hysterically. Only when the mess was over and the lad was consigned back to the fridge did they cease. The medical staff congratulated us and asked if we did Christmas parties and if not to come back soon. We were called Car 54 after that. Occasionally we would call in to see them and be greeted with a 'nudge, nudge, wink, wink, say no more'. Police have to be able to laugh at themselves from time to time.

6

Holden Hill

I transferred to Holden Hill – the old base built before the new complex. This was a very happy environment. Complements of CIB were there and I enjoyed the mix with both styles. Don Hay was there, an ex-RAN man and a very good detective. His mate Trevor Kipling became famous for his involvement in the Family murders.

All good things come to an end: the system was soon changed to a sector system, which provided great police coverage but lousy hours. I was on separate shifts to my wife. That did not promote harmony. The base of operations was then Para Hills headquarters.

Just before I went there, I attended a suicide at Black Top Hill Road, One Tree Hill; a man had gassed himself in his station wagon and had been there for about ten days. The body was on the nose and on retrieving it from the back of the van, a blowfly flew in my mouth. That was the only time I was ever sick on duty. Not a bad start for Christmas Eve 1973.

On Christmas Day, I was off, surprisingly. My family went to my brother-in-law Ralph's house at Fulham Gardens. During dinner I heard a loud bang. Three children knocked on the door and said their mum was dead. Dad had shot her. Ralph and I raced over and the scene that confronted us was a woman with her face gone, brain on the bed intact and her partner rolling in blood but still with a shotgun. Kicking the gun away, I checked if it was loaded by opening the breach; it wasn't. We contained the scene until the arrival of major crime. I later gave evidence in the murder trial. All in all, a Christmas I would rather forget.

Not a good year: my dad Henry Lawrence Clift died, too young, sixty-four years, of a stroke while at his employment. Mum and we were at a loss. I had relied so much on his wisdom and now I was on my own. I guess I grew up quickly in that year.

I was working then on the mixed patrols. This was a male and female uniform set-up; women police only previously dealt with kids. M and I were called to a shop-stealing incident at Ingle Farm. An eighty-five-year-old had been detained for stealing a block of chocolate. My first thought was to take her outside and get her home and pay for the chocolate. I was approaching her when she must have thought she was in for the long drop. She grabbed the giant block of chocolate and ate the lot in front of us. After cautioning her, we took her home. The store chief was pretty cool. She wrote it off and sent a letter to the old lady banning her from the store for a while.

General police were required on most peak periods to assist the traffic control group. There was a situation along King William Street, Adelaide, whereby no right turns were enforced by two police officers at each intersection along the street from 4.15 p.m. till 6 p.m. on Mondays to Fridays. The enforcement was assisted by large 'No Right Turn' signs temporarily placed on brackets high up on the traffic-light pole. Two steps were positioned and the detailed officer would climb the steps, place the signs and then move into the intersection, standing on the south side, moving on any motorists who were deliberately disobeying the signs or inadvertently attempting a right turn.

I was detailed on a Monday night to assist Dave, who would take the first turn. Dave was a bit slow; although I am usually about 180 degrees, I would say he was almost flat-lining. I watched as he climbed the pole with the sign in his hand. Step one was OK; he secured it. The problem began when he started to climb down. Not the most sure-footed person in the force, he was not looking where he was going and was probably fixated on moving into the intersection.

The lights changed to green. A short, small, very elderly lady darted under his feet. Concomitant in point of time, the stumbling Dave's foot plunged onto the small, short old lady's shoulders. Then, losing his balance, he escaped from his pole position and by now had two feet on her shoulders. The small, short old lady made it into the safety area in the middle of the road. With great agility, the balancing man on the top of her shoulders managed to stay upright.

Finally not able to bear the weight of the thirteen-stone police officer, with a huge gasp as the air went from her lungs, she folded into a heap on the road. At the same time as she collapsed, and just before she hit the bitumen, it was with amazement that I saw the balancing fool step off and with a nonchalant look on his face begin to direct traffic. Meanwhile, in a crumpled heap, lay the primary source of the incredible balancing act.

The small, short old lady, with her now-crumpled Miss Marple hat, gradually recovered her cool, stood up and straightened her glasses. A look of recognition came across her face as she spotted a policeman standing nearby. Whether Dave thought silence was golden or he was not about to admit that he had been the second person in the balancing act, I can't say.

She made a quick two-yard dash to Dave and said, 'Did you see a bird or something land on my shoulder just then?'

Dave said 'No', which was, of course, accurate.

She said 'Typical' in a loud voice. 'Cops never around when you need them.'

Dave, the mysterious goony bird, did not reply. There had been a policeman nearby; he just happened to have been standing on her shoulders.

During all of this time I was catching flies with my mouth wide open. The crumpled lady with the crumpled Miss Marple hat merged into the crowd of pedestrians. No report of the incident was ever made.

In 1972 PW and I worked together at Holden Hill. He was the best impressionist I have ever known, on a par with the greats. I was not too bad but he left me for dead. We had many laughs as a team.

Later in life he came to the courts and we continued our repertoire. A full Japanese army uniform was handed in. We intended to donate it to a museum. I tried on the over-shirt and the hat and, as I was not far from home, we drove to pick up my meal. I intended to show my wife, who thought I was mad in any case. PW was driving the vehicle. It was very quiet. PW stopped an elderly driver for a minor traffic breach, intending to caution him. It was dusk. I remained in the car with the hat still plonked on my head.

The old gent followed PW back to our car, too late for me to make a quick change. PW tried to shake him off with some tale and on the motorist's journey to our car I saw an RSL badge on his lapel. I'm in trouble, I thought, trying to shrink down. He made a beeline for me, with PW now asserting that I was on my way to a fancy dress ball.

The old bloke was a New Guinea vet. All he saw in the dark was a Jap sitting in a police vehicle. And he was going to have the last say. When he wrenched open my door, I got out and stood up. He looked stunned. He saw the blue trousers and the black shoes. I bowed, he got it, and he grinned then laughed and walked away shaking his head. Nothing was said.

A week later, my boss, 'Smiler', called me in. He looked at me.

I blurted it out. 'Is this about the Jap uniform?'

He smiled and nodded.

I explained it all, and then he told me that I should apologise to the local RSL. I did. Smiler was there and I made the most of having an enraptured audience.

The old digger came up later and said, 'I give you Corporal Tsanu of the SA Police.'

It caused a bit of a laugh but it could have ended a lot worse. Very embarrassing, though.

You can choose your friends but you can't choose your relatives. Blood is thicker than water. Old clichés but applicable.

In 1973, I was called to an incident at North East Road, Holden Hill. There was a stand-off between a deranged man and the police. Not a siege as such. I was returning to base from my task as an enquiry man. Many summonses had been served and, as an old friend wryly remarked, that means 'Summons in trouble'. A call on the network required my attendance at the scene of the stand-off and I was curious. I spoke to the senior at the scene and he told me that my cousin was the person involved and he had asked for me. I pushed open the door. I saw him, holding a huge axe. He was distraught, dribble running down his face, which was also tear-stained. I spoke to him quietly and he nodded. I noted that most of the furniture in the room had been destroyed, I assumed with axe blows, and I then asked him to give me the axe. He had put on weight since we last met and, at about six foot three inches, gripping an axe tightly, he looked dangerous. I surveyed the room for a possible quick exit if things got worse.

He looked at me askew, turning away slightly. I have seen John Wayne in his movies make a similar action then turn round and strike his adversary. I was prepared, but going for a gun I suddenly realised I didn't have one, so I put out my hand and asked him to give me the axe. He broached the distance between, lowering the axe and handing it to me.

There was a threat implied up till that moment and I decided to take it no further. I commanded him to sit down. He complied.

He broke down, telling me the reason why he had destroyed all of his furniture, crying out in a flood of tears, 'She's given me the pox,' then showing me his arms covered in scabs bearing pus.

His partner then entered. They hugged each other. And suddenly all seemed to be forgiven. I could see no advantage in taking the matter any further and called in the senior and a short chat ensued. His partner did not wish to lodge a complaint even though she had called the police initially. It was his furniture that was damaged. A little bit too much liquor had been consumed by both. He had had a dreadful life as a kid (his father was the army deserter who was flogged). I heard later that he had turned born-again Christian and I believe it worked for him. The whole event could have gone bad and I believe I had some protection on that night…again. Thank God. Which I did. Little did I know that it was GE watching over me.

I was with KN on patrol on night shift checking shops in the area when KN saw a pushbike hidden near the post office. We listened and heard whispered voices coming from the premises. We entered the half-open door. Two males in black with balaclavas were crouched down. They were armed with jimmy bars. We crept out and called for back-up.

Don Hay and Trevor Kipling, the CIB detectives, were there in a flash. We all entered. With bar raised, one of the crooks made a rush towards Don, who blocked his approach. Because of the darkness, I can't say how it happened but the next I saw was the crook flying through the air and landing on a bookcase.

Don, ever cool, said, 'Pick up that man, Cliffy. He's just fallen in the bookshelves.'

Don was later promoted and was a well respected boss. Trevor became a lead man in family murder matters which would have tested the mettle of many a hard-bitten investigator, and I should imagine that the lack of closure in part on those matters would be significantly traumatic and remain with people all of their lives. Needless to say, I have much admiration for Trevor Kipling and all the others involved in that sad aspect of SA crime.

A riot broke out at the Windsor Gardens Hotel car park in 1974. Many police vans were called in and we stood provocatively with the doors open, catching passing punters. Those with big fists and big mouths went in the back. When a van was full, it would be driven to the cop shop and on the way, depending on their behaviour, the driver would speed up and then brake. This would ensure a quieter ride back, most of the punters being dazed.

Chief Inspector ES was the commander and a man with a formidable reputation. Very tall, rock-hard-looking with the appearance of a stockman. Though he spoke with a lisp, his quiet voice had quelled many a riot. The crowds were slowly dispersing and I was engaged in conversation with ES and Inspector JC when I saw a drunken fool lurching towards us with his fists up. I was about to warn ES but he just shook his head. We continued to talk. The drunken fool made his move, moving into ES's personal space under his armpit.

Without halting his conversation, ES reached out with his right arm and brought it down on the hapless fool's head right on the crown. He fell straight down on the bitumen and, still not batting an eyelid, ES said, with his lisp now prominent, 'Shove him in the van, Mr Clift.'

Which I did, though the dead weight of the unconscious man was a bit much. I have never seen such a move since. I hope that man made a life-changing decision to stay away in the future from the armpits of a cop taller than himself.

I have mingled with cops in my twin careers for many years. I feel qualified to attest to the fact that not many go bad. It is amazing that, if a crime is committed and there is a hint of non-compliance on the part of the police, they are the first suspects. When allegations are found to be without any substance, most cops just get on with it, brushing it off but filing it in their heads. Lingering doubts remain that the public just do not trust us. I encountered a serious side of this at Holden Hill in 1974. That occasion left me in doubt from then on, and always on my guard.

On the night in question, I was on patrol and called to a job, a possible siege at Valley View. It was a familiar address and I knew the people there. Constable JB had asked for me to attend, upon request of the wife at that address. I knew their family situation. We had all got on well, or so I had thought, and I knew that he had a habit of bashing her. She would not make a complaint.

I looked at her swollen face, cut lips and closed eyes and said, 'He's gone too far this time, J.'

She agreed. We sent her to hospital. The second reason I was called was she said he had an old .410 shotgun and would shoot anyone who came in.

I called out to him and he said, 'Think you're bloody Division 4.' (*Division 4* was a TV cop show at the time.)

I yelled out, 'Open it or I'll break it down.'

I heard shuffling and GB, my partner, and I kicked the door in just as I saw him shoving an old gun in the manhole. He jumped down and raced to the kitchen with us in hot pursuit. I collared him at the fridge, wrapped him up in a bear hug, and we both fell down, pulling the fridge on top of us, spilling out all its contents. We finally subdued him, angry now, with a mouthful of McCain's frozen peas, then handcuffed him and took him to the cop shop. He was charged, searched and placed in a cell, where he ranted for a while. We went back on duty. There were other jobs to do.

He was bailed in the morning and I was not present. I was woken about 8 a.m. by an inspector telling me I had been accused of stealing the man's watch at the time he was bailed. I was suspended from duty. I ranted. I thought it all out and rang a detective I knew. He went straight to the new bailing sergeant's office. He found that in the morning the sergeant had bailed two people, at the same time tipping out their property on the desk. One of the crooks was a smart thief. V, the detective, went to his house and arrested him for larceny and my complainant was given his watch back. There were no apologies from the sergeant, whom I called a bloody idiot the next day.

The matter came to court. The defendant's wife relented and withdrew her complaint. He was convicted on charges of resisting arrest and possessing an illegal firearm. It was not loaded at the time. They walked out arm in arm and outside he tossed a half-baked apology.

All I said was 'You ought to get some more food in the fridge for the kids.' It went over his head. I am eternally grateful to Detective V.

7

Prosecution

Before promotion, I was posted to the prosecution branch. We would peruse reports and check before they were sent on to the prosecutors who would present them to court. It was a busy time but I learned a lot about the law.

I had been there for some time when my boss told me to report to the new big boss, which I did. We all stayed out of his way. He was almost a genius and on a different plane to the rest of us.

I knocked on his door. No response. I opened it slightly to be greeted by a huge law book being flung at head height towards me. I ducked it and counter-punched it, sending it flying back, and it fell on the floor.

The big boss said, 'Great punch, LC.' He then threw another smaller book.

I was closer this time. He was standing but not for long. It struck him on the head, knocking off his hat and sending him to the floor. There he sat on the book, and I stood looking at him with my reddening knuckles.

He said, 'What now?'

I said, looking down at him seated on the book on the floor having retrieved his hat, placed on back to front, 'I'm not LC.'

He replied, not unlike James Cagney in *Mr Roberts*, 'Then who are you?'

I said, 'I'm Ray Clift.'

He paused, still seated on the book.

I broke the ice. I asked him if he wished me to send in LC, adding 'Sir' appropriately.

He nodded.

I left the office and told LC, an inoffensive man with a dry sense of humour. Now forewarned, he approached the office of the big one with a wire basket on his head. He was invited in. He made an attempt to remove the basket but was told to leave it on. He sat there for a full fifteen minutes being berated by the big boss.

My boss asked LC what the chief had wanted.

LC replied, 'Stuffed if I know. He was sitting on the floor with his hat on back to front and I was wearing a wire basket on my head all the time. I couldn't hear a word.'

Did Alice fall through a rabbit hole? I sometimes wonder.

Apart from two other murders and endless arrests, 1974 went by and by 1975 I was promoted to sergeant second grade and took a posting at Region T (traffic). My boss, an inspector, a former Norwood league player, a coach and police football coach, a ruthless prosecutor, kept a watchful eye on me. He was a personable no-nonsense man who commanded respect.

It was a delicate environment. I gained respect by listening and endeavoured to ensure that the policies of SAPOL were carried out, as well as being a sort of counsellor to less senior people. Speed cops are a pretty good group to manage; they are old hands, not frightened to speak out, able to work with minimum supervision. Anyone trying to lord it over them usually came unstuck. I used a bit of manipulation, occasional mild blackmail, but kept a good memory, not forgetting any good works done. It seemed to work.

I and Brian Hughes were now the administrative senior sergeants for traffic at Para Hills base in charge of the speed cops, who had been decentralised to the suburbs.

Col Kain was the traffic chief there. He had been a top police boxer and for some reason had the nickname of Grassy. He wasn't like any boss I ever knew, very clever and a laughing jokey bloke.

On one of the parade musters, I called out all the names, turned to Col and announced all present and correct. While saluting, my hat fell off. I bent down to pick it up, so did he, and his hat fell off. We had each other's hats on and then began a perfect hat exchange like one I saw in an old Laurel and Hardy movie. Then one of the troops snuck a moving phallic-symbol vibrator onto the floor. The object rotated around the room. Grassy announced that one member, the vibrator, was incorrectly dressed. Just imagine how that brought the house down. Grassy was a champ.

I filled in on a Sunday morning for a general duties sergeant. It was quiet. I was catching up on paperwork when a call came through about a siege at Salisbury Heights. A supervisor was required. I rapidly got there. Star Force was not available; we were it. The householder inside had tied his wife up, gagged her and fired shots into a mirror.

Looking through the window, I could see he was on the lounge holding a sawn-off .22 rifle – a dangerous weapon. One of my speed cops, Steve Rix, walked in the front door with me. I was unarmed. We sized up the situation. The man was draped across the lounge chair, the .22 still clutched in his hands. I thought, well, here goes. I slid around as carefully as I could, then sprang on him, grabbing the rifle and wrenching it away. Steve took it; it was loaded. The woman was freed and we frogmarched the defendant outside. It was the longest twenty feet I have ever walked.

Steve and I received awards later. The man was deported. The worse thing was that he was suffering from hepatitis A, so I and my whole family had to attend hospital and receive the huge gamma injection. All in a day's work, eh? My daughter at times reminds me of the pain of those injections, adding, 'Thanks, Dad.'

I was on supervision duties in the Elizabeth area at 11.40 p.m. on

---

THE SOUTH AUSTRALIAN POLICE GAZETTE   October 19, 1977

ERRATUM
(See Organisational Changes *P.G.* page 87/77)

Communications Research—Superintendent C. G. Wilson should read Communications Services—Superintendent C. G. Wilson.

P.C.O., 3/2/340180.

SPECIAL MENTION

A Special Mention is awarded to Inspector K. D. Moran for displaying leadership, physical courage and devotion to duty reflecting credit on the Force when arresting a mentally unstable man for assault at Morphett Vale on the 6th September, 1977.

The Inspector strategically deployed personnel to seal off the house, which was in darkness and occupied by the man who was believed to be armed and alone. By maintaining persuasive conversation with the man as he calmly and quietly approached the open side door of the house the Inspector was able to finally get close enough to the man and overpower him. A large carving knife was located near the door where the man was standing.

P.C.O., 44/2/340586.

SPECIAL MENTION

A Special Mention is awarded to Sergeant First Grade Clift, R. J. L., 1210/6, and Constable Rix, S. C., 2436/5, for displaying physical courage and devotion to duty reflecting credit on the Force when disarming a deranged man in his home at Salisbury Heights on the 14th August, 1977.

Both members entered the house occupied by only the deranged person, who was sitting on a bed armed with a loaded sawn-off .22 calibre rifle, and sobbing profusely. Just prior to their entry the man had fired three shots into a large mirror in the room. Sergeant Clift, closely followed by Constable Rix, quietly and slowly approached the man and disarmed him without a struggle.

P.C.O., 44/2/340262.

LEGIBILITY OF ACCIDENT REPORTS—FOR MICROFILM

Members are again reminded to ensure that Accident Reports are prepared in a clear and legible type to assist in the microfilming process. Accident Reports submitted in faint type are of no use and will be returned to the station of origin for retyping.

Reference: *Police Gazette*, page 68 of 1974.

P.C.O., 11/1/289557.

By Authority: D. J. WOOLMAN, Government Printer, South Australia

Monday 2 August 1976. I received a call to attend a house in the area where a man was threatening police with a knife. Three police vehicles were there, along with an ambulance. I knew all of the personnel who were present, mostly old hands who knew their stuff. I saw Greg Hooper talking to a man in the kitchen. There was a considerable distance between them. The man was armed with a knife and had slash wounds on his wrists. Blood was on the floor. He was yelling 'Pigs out' repeatedly. It looked as though he would soon lunge at Greg. He dropped the knife and Greg, a raw-boned athlete and a good sportsman, immediately acted. He sprang the distance almost totally in the air, landing on the hapless man. I followed him instantly and we subdued the man, holding him down. He was arrested and later charged. Greg went on later to be a detective well known in the south-east.

Late in 1976 I was travelling north along Bridge Road at Para Hills conveying a police car to that base. Two officers were in a lead vehicle just ahead. On the left was an open area, now mallee, known as Para Paddocks. I heard a noise like a gunshot and then saw the lead vehicle stop. Officers alighted and then yelled, 'Someone's shooting at us' as more shots were fired. Two bullet holes were in the front left side of their car. We all ducked down on the right side. It was very dark.

One of the cops radioed in and gave our situation to the network. A quick response was received from the duty CIB car and they were soon on the way. It seemed an eternity, crouched down behind the car with shots still being fired at us. Then a message came over: 'We got him.'

I soon spoke to the senior CIB officer, a detective inspector, a paradox of a man: an academic genius with a real streak of a laconic Australian and an ex RAAF man later to become the boss of the Nuriootpa police base. DI told me that both of the CI men crept up without any cover over a fair distance and then rushed the man and arrested him. He was a sniper armed with a deadly Hornet rifle. DI said that he could have picked us off at any time if he wished. I never found out the reason for his actions and I hope that the two CI men received some recognition for their brave act.

In 1980 at Para Hills base at the close of a shift, I was talking to a male senior sergeant when we heard the loud noise of gunfire in the front office. Rushing out, we spotted a small woman loading a .410 shotgun. The target of her hatred was her ex-husband, who had smartly ducked down, but she was going to have another go. Ian and I restrained her and disarmed her. We sent the poor sod of a cop home and kept her in the back office. The hole in the rear of the office wall was obvious.

About five minutes later, the shift boss asked us if it had been quiet. When I told him about the incident, he stood there in amazement. I told him that she was loopy and nothing much could be done. I suggested that a mixed patrol take her home. We arranged some medical treatment the next day. He, being a common-sense sort of bloke, agreed. The wall was plastered up. The gun was handed in and destroyed.

About two nights later, the same boss called me in about a defect that a taxi driver was complaining about. I quickly looked outside and saw the defect, for bald tyres, allotted to the vehicle by my blokes. Seemed correct. The boss told me to fix it as it was a traffic man who issued it. I walked into his office. There was a fellow I knew from the old Holden Hill days. One would call him a litigant now. But I knew a bit about this fellow; for instance, when he had a lot of debt, he advertised his two children for sale. A bit nutty, you could say. He looked at me, saw the stripes, opened his mouth and closed it.

I said, 'Well, well, well...how you going? Still advertising your kids for sale?'

No reply.

I said, 'I've had a look at the defect. I suggest by tomorrow you get a set of proper tyres. Do you understand me?'

He walked out. End of complaint.

The boss said, 'How did you do it, sergeant?'

I said, 'Empty cans make the most noise, inspector.'

I was heavily involved during this period – for a second time – with the army reserve and served fifteen years with the Military Police and Army Intelligence (INT), as well as talking and writing to GE. INT is a fascinating thought-probing section and I regretted when the age limit forced my retirement later on. Most people would imagine that it is full of right-wing hawks. That is a misconception. An intelligence person needs to keep a balance and assess situations whether a commander likes it or not. Sycophants do not fit well in intelligence sections.

That break from normal police work helped to heal the wounds of my marriage break-up. 1981 and 1982 were my desert years. I was working in

Adelaide for a short time when my friend from traffic control days, now stationed at the quaint Torrens Lake police station, sent an invitation in the mail to my posting. It was an invitation to lunch, asking if I could try to get some time off and attend. Mick and his wife were good friends and good cooks, so I was not about to pass it up and asked my boss if I could take an hour for lunch and make it up at the end of my shift, and he gave permission. I attended at the small station, yards away from where I was working, and was greeted at the front door by Mick wearing a chef's hat and an apron over his uniform. A 'gone to lunch' sign was hung on the front door.

We both found the situation ludicrous but, always good on the fang then, I looked forward to what was on offer and it was not long in coming. While he was heating the meal, his hat slipped slightly and Mick, with a humour I shall always treasure, and an accent and style not unlike Michael Palin, regaled me with some of his tales from his days in the Irish guards driving a tank in Korea. Not exactly the safest spot in the world at that time.

A knock came on the front door just as he was about to serve what smelled like a goulash, accompanied by a dry white. He opened the door and I heard the quizzical voice of a man somewhat concerned at Mick's apparel ask, 'Is this the police station?'

Always the gentleman, Mick invited him in without further ado and said, 'Had lunch?'

'No' was the reply.

I stood up and shook the man's hand and he was invited to sit down. We were all treated to a great meal with home-cooked bread. We started to giggle about the situation and the man soon latched onto the great understated sense of humour from our chef. Mick had to keep adjusting his ridiculously oversize hat, which flopped to one side like a dog with a dropped ear.

The gent had to ask. I could see the words forming on his lips. Excessively politely, he enquired, 'Is this how SA Police treats all its clients?'

We assured him that it was not. He left a happy man. I wrote down his details and reported the minor incident at the end of my shift. He probably still tells the story.

On a warm afternoon in the early 1980s, I was driving to my base at

Holden Hill, when a call came through for assistance. I recognised the voice of the sergeant involved, AC. I entered the driveway on foot, looked over a high fence and saw AC sitting on a garden seat. Two metres from him and opposite was a younger man very distraught and holding a .410 shotgun at high port diagonally. A dangerous weapon in close quarters. Other police had arrived and were outside the fence. AC signalled for me to come in. I walked in and sat down alongside him. A dialogue was engaged in between the three of us. It was a family violence situation with all the inherent elements of danger. AC had been there for some time talking the man down and I guessed with the heat he was feeling quite jaded.

In about ten minutes, the man dropped the firearm parallel to the ground. I looked at AC and we just reached over quietly and took the weapon without any resistance. It was loaded. The outside back-up moved in and a non-violent arrest was made.

I told my boss the next day and he remarked, 'Yes, .410s are popular and I've taken quite a few off defendants.' He had seen much country service, frequently on his own, and certainly would have encountered that type of incident.

In the high summer of 1983, the threatening summer skies, with raging north winds and 40°C or more heat each day, weighed on the southern states of Australia, with one of the worst bushfire seasons ever encountered in the country. South Australia, and in particular the heavy wooded areas of the Mount Lofty Ranges, were on high fire alert. Fires were breaking out through the ranges. Traffic and general police were deployed to assist in diversion and at times provide safe routes for Emergency vehicles.

In the foothills of Adelaide at Anstey's Hill, a water resources depot is situated on the high side of a valley. I was detailed to spot fires at this location and report any sightings to a command post. I was issued with powerful binoculars. As a metropolitan fire service officer nearby with a giant hose was playing water around on the nearby foliage, the situation seemed fairly safe for us. I could see fires in the distance approaching and the wind was very strong. To my left there was a smoky haze about ten metres away. Momentarily distracted, I heard a loud crackling noise. I looked to the left. Breaking out of the haze was a thirty-metre wall of flame rapidly approaching, no more than six metres away. I yelled out to the fireman, who spotted the terrifying sight. He immediately turned round and ran towards me. We both ran like gazelles. I could feel the heat on my back, almost singeing my hair. We fled into the concrete building and lay low as the wall of flame passed over. The flame added ash and debris to the smoke we had already inhaled. Other workmen who were in the building looked terrified and were all deathly silent.

The whole episode lasted no more than seconds. I would have to say the terror of it still remains. This was a close-to-death scenario. We were very lucky. One rolled ankle, one trip on our rush back to the building, would have seen the last of us. Interestingly, my police vehicle, although covered in ash, was not badly damaged, but a water resources vehicle nearby was in bad shape. My instincts now on high alert to protection from beyond the veil were confirmed after another chat with GE.

We all attended at a St John depot later and after an eye wash were sent home suffering from smoke inhalation. My admiration of fire control people, both regular and casual, has never waned.

I was not alone in the situation I found myself in; many of my speed cops faced similar dangers. I am aware of some unrecognised heroic actions by them on that day, a day I hope to never see again. On that black day I felt a presence, a presence that made my feet connect in a manner that propelled my body to safety.

My mother Ivy May Clift died in April of the year 1985 at age seventy-one. She had been born during World War I and had seen the poverty and sadness of that era in the eastern suburbs of Adelaide. People of her ilk struggled even then, before the Great Depression. Her family's struggles were mostly due to her father's alcoholism. Ivy, being the eldest of six children, would have been a great help to her mother. People must have accepted their poverty and indeed worn it like a badge of courage, and Ivy was no different. Living through the Depression, meeting and marrying Henry Lawrence Clift, must have been like a load lifted from her shoulders. Henry, mainly called Harry, was from Anglo-Irish stock. His family were farmers, hence his love of the land. They were genteel people, well mannered, and they had an air about them.

After Harry's sudden death, Ivy struggled with her grief for the rest of her life. Her co-dependence on Harry made her life without him hard for her to bear. She still got up each morning, in spite of poor health, and battled through each day with crippling arthritis. Many times throughout the eleven years, I thought we would lose her. Her passing was expected, but nevertheless a shock. I believe she knew it was to be soon. She told me of a stash of cash under her mattress. I was to retrieve it and distribute it. I was called to her senior's flat on the morning of her death. I sat and spoke to her where she lay. I told her again about the discovery of my birth. How I wished I had not travelled that road.

The next day I was cleaning up in the flat with some help from my one of my daughters and their mother. After they had gone, I was at the kitchen sink when I felt a cold shiver. I turned around and saw Mum standing there. She did not look happy; then in an instant she stepped towards me and passed right through. That is when I grieved for all the ways that I could have helped her but had not. I would say I was conscience-stricken. I guess I feel that way today. Do not ask me why. Countless attendances at the Spiritualist Church always gave the message that Mum and Dad were happy. I guess I have to let it go at that. GE also reiterated those words.

For South Australia, 1986 was the year of the Jubilee – 150 years since its birth. Many events were arranged. At that time I was a traffic special event coordinator. Plans had to be drawn up, staff had to be organised. Events such as the grand prix, Bay to Birdwood rally, air show and royal family visit took up some time.

Kev Johnson organised the Elizabeth side of the events in his customary dedicated and efficient manner, ensuring that the events went without a hitch. I met all the royal family for a second time and also met His Holiness the Pope on his visit to North Adelaide. He lined up all the speed cops in his entourage and gave each one a personal memento, not enquiring if they were Christian, Protestant or whatever. Close up, he was a serene-looking man.

The years were rolling on – within five years I would be retired from the police force. Kerry, my eldest, was well into a social work career. Jo worked in various jobs at that time.

Those moments that can change our lives are marked on our psyche and remain indelible. They can be instructive or destructive and are nearly always sitting at the back of our brains, returning in spades at times. That scenario is ever present in the life of a police officer. Most encounter that prospect sooner or later. Many get over it – on the surface, that is – depending on the severity and its impact. They are fortunate if that pivotal moment involving violence, whether physical or emotional, passes them by.

It did not pass by a friend of mine on Saturday 12 April 1986 at 4.15 a.m. Now retired and anonymous, B, then a sergeant on solo uniform patrols, spotted an erratically driven vehicle on Main North Road. B, the career cop with experience oozing out of him, was respected by all, a careful, dedicated cop born at Tailem Bend and with that raw-boned look of a former country boy. He stopped the vehicle for a check and noted that there were five occupants. The driver, an Aboriginal youth in his midteens, alighted from the Holden. In conversation with the now agitated man, B noted a broken quarter-window on the vehicle, always a sign then of a stolen vehicle. I will let B tell the story.

> The driver was agitated and started to walk back to the Holden. I followed him back. He opened the front right door and jumped in behind the steering wheel. I could see he was going to drive off. He started the car engine. I asked him for the keys. Four occupants were standing nearby. I reached in the window and grabbed the offender around the upper body. He immediately accelerated. I could not move off while I was hanging on. He increased speed to my estimation of forty to forty-five kilometres an hour. I was being dragged along the road at the same time.
>
> He veered to the right, the car mounting a kerb with me still hanging on. The vehicle, by then on the incorrect side of the road, collided head on with a stobie pole, later found to be bent by the impact. I was thrown about five metres onto the roadway with the force of that impact, during the flight taking the right side door with me. I was stunned, prone, and I heard the noise of an engine revving loudly stuck against the pole. I could not move. The offender sprang on me, kicking me twice in the face. His accomplices had run off. He then knelt on me, raining punches with his fist into my face, and then gouging my eyes with his fingers. I was able to bite his fingers in self-defence. He then bit me on the left upper arm. The scars are prominent.
>
> He broke free and I was still able to tackle him and pull him to the ground. I was determined in spite of my injuries and fatigue now arising to detain him for his crimes. It was a struggle by then to hold him. Breaking free, he ran off. My injuries were visible to all and I was treated at hospital for them. He was eventually arrested and served time in gaol.

I have painted a visual scene encapsulated in the matter of seconds, seconds which might have brought death to B and yet he is still nonchalant, with that air of 'it goes with the job'. That offender was a maniac who did not care about life or property. I doubt that he would have cared if murder had been the charge, so one cannot blame the police if they do not care about that type. B received no commendation for his dogged determination to bring an outrageous offender to justice. Perhaps his nonchalant attitude kept it low profile. He was highly regarded by his senior officers and it is hard to fathom how any commendations slipped through the cracks. That can happen at times. B is certainly not complaining about it even though he still bears the scars of that violent confrontation. Hamlet in his famous speech discussing the afterlife ended with 'Thus conscience doth make cowards of us all.'

Five years later, the station sergeant on duty on Tuesday 19 December 2000 at Holden Hill was B. He picked up his phone to answer a call referred to him. A male person on the other end of the line lived in Newcastle in NSW and the call was from that city. The caller stated he was pissed but had a good memory. He asked for Detective Sergeant C. He was told by B that that officer retired some two years go. Nevertheless, he persisted. He told a story that he and an accomplice in 1995 had committed robberies on banks and a post office. They had fled with cash. B recorded the comprehensive details given by the man. Keeping him on the line talking, B summoned his two officers to take note of what he was writing. Senior Constable JM and the other officer made immediate enquiries. It took some time but it came up accurate. B had on the phone the offender who had carried out the robberies.

The NSW police were contacted. A fax was sent to them confirming the details. The man confessed to it all and was later extradited to SA, where he received a long sentence. B had been on the phone for hours. The man believed that a retired sergeant was still after him. It had haunted him.

It would be easy to dismiss this as all in a day's work. A lazier man might have just dismissed it as a drunken man's bragging. Not B; he followed it through and a cold case was closed. I have not heard of a similar incident. The accounts branch would have shuddered when they saw the phone bill.

I was fortunate enough to be part of the police contingent at the protest over uranium at Roxby Downs. It was two weeks up and two weeks back at Woomera and Roxby. I wouldn't have missed the experience for the world. In attendance at most protests, I found many of the protesters to be genuine. What we didn't appreciate was the 'rent-a-crowd'.

On the winding down at Roxby, I was drinking after duty with the Starries (Star Force) and some Mounties. One of the Starries, due to over-indulgence, brought out a police horse. He proceeded to interview the horse with a microphone. The horse actually seemed to respond, whinnying, stomping his feet and laughing. The Starry was asking funny and ridiculous questions. The horse was inspired by the frequent swigs of VB he received. It was videotaped and was hilarious, the funniest scene I have ever seen with man and horse.

The commander of the whole operation was a brilliant, handsome officer, a former West Torrens league footballer of some fame. He was probably the best South Australian, if not Australian, leader and coordinator of these operations. He knew how to get the best out of his people. Barry was his able energetic deputy. He was a major in the Army Reserves to boot.

After that exercise, sergeants were called to the deputy's office; he had a video he was to display. On it was a team from Holden Hill, having some choir practice after a breakfast. There was some fool dressed as a Rocky Horror character and some others in drag, all pissed. The deputy was horrified and went on about it, berating all the sergeants. Most of us could barely contain ourselves. We all got outside and really broke up. On the way home we were singing, 'Damn it, Janet' and 'Touch me, touch me'. I think a sergeant was charged with allowing liquor to be partaken on police premises.

I volunteered for an army exercise titled Op Red Centre, with the Army Engineers. It was really a survey, including a check on water reserves along the Ghan track. We crossed the Finke and each night stopped, fed, lit campfires and retired to pup tents, off at 7 a.m. for the next leg.

One night about 9 p.m. we were sitting around a campfire made with sleepers from the old track. It had been a long day. Some had gone to sleep on their chairs millionaires. The empty chair alongside was suddenly and quietly occupied by a young full-blood Aboriginal with paint, spears and feathers. I guessed he was on a tribal mission. I was not wrong. More impressive was that he spoke better English than the rest of us. He introduced himself as Bill. He was a member of the North Force Aboriginal Reserve Unit in Darwin. He had seen the fire and had decided to call in for a chat. I asked Bill if he wanted a drink, because we had some private stock. He asked for a Bacardi and Coke, which we had.

I said, 'Why not a beer, Bill?'

He said in his drawl, 'Tops up the white, Ray.' He left as quietly as he came.

*

Traffic had again been reorganised. Time to go do something else. In 1991 I retired and a group farewell was organised at a local hotel. On 17 June 1991 I joined the Courts Administration Authority as a sheriff's officer, though not before I had a chat with GE, because it was a major change in my life. I was in fact going from King of the Hill with forty speed cops under my control to a sheriff's officer without the worry of staff. It was a hands-on job and I knew I would easily be able to work till I was seventy, which I did.

Me: Am I taking the right turn, GE?

GE: Yes. It has been in your mind for some time. A lot less stress.

Me: Will it lead to anything I desire?

GE: What do you desire?

Me: Something which will develop the arts side of me.

GE: Shuffle your tarot cards. See what they come up with.

I did and it suggested writing. The six of cups predicted, 'Go back to an old skill.'

8

Sheriff's Officer

At that time, the Sheriff's Office engaged personnel to staff courts. (Police were detailed to sit in on all courts as the orderly, an arrangement that changed in 1982, when the service was civilianised.)

It was a busy day in the Elizabeth Court. I was the runner. I would manage bails and bonds, see that they were signed. A punter named M was aggressive and was refusing to wait in the court. I had told him on numerous occasions to settle down. My patience was running thin. He stood in the dock scowling and back-chatting the senior magistrate (SM). He was given bail and told to wait in court on the chairs opposite and I could see he was not going to comply. I blocked his exit. He called me an old fart. He tried ducking. I grabbed both arms and held them out the side, stepped to the left and then waltzed him backwards across the court room not unlike a quickstep. I thrust him down on the chair. I had had enough of him by then.

I did my best impression of Clint Eastwood but forgot the lines, just saying, 'Punk.'

He sat there eyeballing me.

I took him to the JP to sign the papers but he ran out. I grabbed his jacket on the way out and I knew he would have to come back for it. He did and while I was standing there holding his jacket he walked in, treating me like a valet, placing his two arms in the jacket.

I almost threw him in the JP's office and when he left he yelled out, 'I'll get you, dickhead.'

Using an old cliché and not fast enough on the day I yelled back, 'You and what army?' I am ashamed that I had not a better cliché on that day.

The court giggled at our quickstep.

One of the police orderlies in 1982, possibly the last, was a card named FK. On the case he was attending to, the SM dismissed a case of indecent language, concluding that the F word was at times not offensive. The SM remarked that it was heard in many places and he was not offended by it. FK was, and at the end of the session he was required to call out the names of the non-appearances. FK complied, was sworn in by the clerk and as usual gave his name, occupation and then called the names of defendants who had not appeared.

At the conclusion, he stated in a loud voice, looking directly at the SM, 'And there were no fucking appearances, Your Honour.'

The SM, himself a humorist, paused and said, 'I guess I asked for that, FK.'

The court orderly's job in 1991 when I joined was staffed by many ex-police and ex-armed forces personnel. For obvious reasons, the hierarchy felt that they could all handle themselves; they were compliant and punctual. That worked very well then, but times changed and soon many occupations were recruiting, regardless of gender, sexual preferences or whatever. The changes made interesting challenges. In most cases it was a rewarding experience.

Our roles were expanded, the pay improved. The training supplied then was excellent. I learnt a lot from the youngsters, all computer-literate; it was a fresh approach. I still miss most of my mates from the Elizabeth Court.

The Elizabeth Magistrates Court serviced a large area of the northern districts of Adelaide. A woman by the name of Janet Morrison, a Sandra Bullock lookalike, became a good friend; I had served under her father, 'Darkie' Collins. Janet was talking to Kerry, an Aboriginal youth worker, at the end of a youth court day.

Charlie, our Welsh orderly and a top bowler, and naturally a singer, was going home and called out to Kerry, 'See you, Darkie.'

Janet was horrified, but still a wry smile creased her lips when Kerry called out, 'Yeah, see you, Charlie.'

Our Aboriginal staff were in good hands. All had a laugh at the innocent remark.

Most days in the general court, there are between twenty and twenty-five custodies in the upstairs court cells, where they are interviewed by their lawyers. When called up to appear, they are ushered into court by the privatised GSL service. This adds to the trauma of the day, with hordes of relatives packing the court to glimpse their incarcerated kinfolk. It can be emotionally charged. Most of the orderlies are just like cops; they grumble, grizzle and still have a good laugh at the end of the day.

I was the second orderly in a busy court one day with John Bird, a Vietnam vet, a real character. I was busy obtaining files from counsel at the Bar table when I heard a whining noise from behind. I turned round and saw a disabled gent in a motorised wheelchair about six feet away. I tried to jump out of the way; it was too late. The occupant, in his driven desire to reach the prison dock, picked me up on the way. There I was locked in a maniacal embrace with the occupant, both trying hard to stop the now out of control machine, as the joystick came off in my hand, and we were by then circulating around what spare space was available. I finally made a shoulder roll onto the court floor. The court was by then in an uproar, people screeching with laughter. The SM took off out the back and I could hear his laughter reverberating down the corridor. John Bird had ducked down in the orderlies' station, laughing so loud that snot was running out of his nose.

I had by then contained myself and said, 'Bloody big help you were, John.'

Which brought forth more shrieking.

The second time I made a fool of myself was at the Clare Court on a debtors' day. The courts are closed, for privacy reasons, to all but the participants. I was asked to bring in number 16. I went to the foyer and called his name. As he approached, he slipped, seemed to faint and fell down on top of me. I checked to see if he was all right and quickly sent in the next person, number 17. The court judicial officer quietly enquired what had happened to number 16.

Still flustered and not thinking of the consequences, I called out, 'He went down on me in the foyer.' I stopped, realising the implications.

It was too late by now. Counsel and the clerk, and the judicial officers, were by then in fits of laughter. I really knew then I should have stayed in bed that day. When it all settled down, Peter, one of the lawyers, asked me if there was any foreplay beforehand.

Elizabeth Debtors Court can be depressing. Largely the debts are self-inflicted because of the sheer volume of easy credit available. That in itself is a millstone around the neck of people who have no concept of budgeting. Most of the people spend more than they earn. Many of them never recover. Some, if they are buying a house, owe three years of council rates. The poker machines in the area are full of people in huge debt, hoping to win money to pay off debts. They become addicted and are driven further down the debt ladder. Most are appearing in court to get the best deal they can, to reduce fortnightly payments. They sit quietly awaiting their time in court, to hopefully achieve their best result. When called in, one at a time, they are able to explain to the registrar what their opposition is. Many are in tears at the end of their appearance. The sheriff's officer calls them in order of the time of their attendance. Unless the officer is told otherwise, that rule is strictly adhered to.

On one occasion, a rather slovenly-looking man arrived at about 10.30 a.m., an hour and a half late. He demanded to go in straight away. I enquired why he needed to jump the queue. He replied he had a job interview. On looking at his appearance and noting the thongs, I quietly asked if his previous place of work had an unemployed lion-tamer. When I quickly saw he didn't get it, I told him I had no authority to place him above the others. Each time I went to the foyer to call another customer, he was making loud noises and bagging me. I thought then, next time I'm out and you open your gob, mate, I'm going for you. Next time out, I was again harassed by the disruptive gent.

I finally said, 'Look, there's only one person who can let you jump the list."

He was sucked in and asked, 'Who?'

I replied, 'God.' I looked up at the ceiling and, in a loud voice with arms outstretched, said, 'God, can you help this man get in now?'

Silence.

The man looked at me and I said in my best Southern preacher voice, 'Ah cannot help you, brother. God, he doesn't answer.'

A giant biker waiting quietly to go in said to the fellow, 'Sit down, dickhead, and wait your turn.'

Naturally, the man was the last one in at the end of the session.

Mondays in the packed Elizabeth Magistrates Court were emotionally charged times: the weekend arrests, the relatives hanging about, winding their hankies in knots, stressing about how long it would take for their partner to be bailed. Many of the arrested clients appeared before the domestic violence court. Those matters were dealt with individually.

I had obtained the names of all appearing. I ushered Mark into the dock, where he stood head bowed, face tear-stained, as the prosecutor read out the allegations.

The duty lawyer spoke for him. 'He has a job, Your Honour, a mortgage, a family, children he loves. He regrets the incident and I suggest a report for the next appearance,' were his final remarks. He entered a guilty plea.

The matter was dealt with. He received a suspended sentence. We chatted while he waited for his papers to sign.

Mark appeared two months later in custody. He had breached the conditions. He was gaoled for seven months in Yatala. I played minder until the van arrived and he freely and candidly told me of his fall from grace. His job had gone due to absenteeism and medication. His family had gone. Bored at home, he started to play the pokies. He would play back winnings, hoping for more. Bordering then on an addiction to alcohol, and with the gambling hook well stuck in place, he forged his wife's name on a $10,000 loan. This was soon gobbled up. Now in panic, awaiting the knock on the door from the police, he stole his mate's lawnmower, sold it to a second-hand dealer for a pittance, and then waited the arrival of the police. That knock soon came and he was arrested. He made restitution to his wife by not claiming his share of the house. The house was sold, with the loan money being paid out.

The grapevine told me that upon his release he had straightened up and was on the mend. That information was incorrect and it was confirmed when I saw him some time later near a shopping centre. He looked terrible and a sour pungent odour surrounded his body. I engaged him in a short conversation, avoiding any talk of his kids. I spoke directly about his addictions.

He replied in a croaky voice, 'I get my dole money, I blow it on the pokies. Then I get food from Anglicare.'

I saw the two bags he was carrying. I saw his thongs, his blue toes. It was a cold day. I said, 'Where do you live?'

He shivered slightly, with those frail shoulders that once held some muscle. He looked up. I saw some moisture forming in the corner of his eyes. I scanned his face. He was struggling to give me a response. The body language told me he acknowledged my empathy for his condition but he wished to leave himself with some dignity.

A slight cheeky grin creased the corners of his mouth, which then manifested into a radiant smile, a smile that almost disarmed the female SM who had sentenced him. His scratchy voice replied softly, 'Wherever, mate…wherever.'

A protracted silence followed. I finally broke that silence. I reached out, clutching the shaking hand. The smell of the unkempt man was not then relevant and in the shaking of that cold clammy hand I was still stuck for words but they tumbled out anyway. I said, 'Take care, mate. Take care.'

In silent acceptance, now wiping a tear-stained face, he nodded, speechless, turning around heavily, and then stumbled away with his food parcels held fast to his body and occasionally wiping his eyes, lifting the bag in order to do so.

I walked towards my car, our second car, fumbling with the coins in my pocket, the keys in my other hand, at age sixty-nine still in good health… I opened the car door and sat for a time in contemplation of Mark, of all the addicts I had met in my life, of Turp, and the tough shell I had acquired over all those years. Yet Mark had got to me. I drove away, adjusted the rear-vision mirror, looked in it and said softly to myself, 'It's a fine line, isn't it? A very fine line.'

9

Career's End

My career in the Sheriff's Office came to a close on 7 July 2006, and I was the guest at a gathering of many friends.

Did I choose the script of my life before entering the life of Raymond J.L. Clift? Reincarnation devotees suggest that that is the case. Millions of people on this planet believe in that hypothesis. I can only speculate on that matter but have a view which is backed up by GE, who has told me we were together in the US as tribesmen, which seems to be a credible scenario for souls.

Writing has always been a labour of love for me. The sheer concentration of it immediately places the writer in the moment. In that moment, the process of past examination is part of the process of placing one firmly in the now. It has certainly filled the mental gap between retirement and now. I certainly recommend it to older folks, if it is only for family records. That process of appreciation of the moment can bring on a personal epiphany, a reinforcement of how precious being in the now is. If I am not writing, I am reading, walking and weight training. The absorption of the physical exercise certainly forces one to deep breathe the oxygen life force we all require. My fascination with spiritual matters has never waned.

Is it publish and be damned or do your writings languish in some cold case awaiting discovery that may fall on the shoulders of a descendant? I imagine that descendant finding a dusty trunk with a dusty collection of unpublished manuscripts. And I visualise him or her sitting back, flicking through the discovery and then finding a comfortable chair in a warm spot digesting the material (metaphorically, that is) and, at the end of that discourse, proclaiming incredulously, 'Did great great grandfather write all that?'

Hopefully at that point, the long-dead writer will, with a pocket of cold air and a wispy materialisation, whisper in the reader's ear these words: 'Yes, child, I did, but it didn't seem much at the time.'

*

I have tried to present a human face of the police and the pitfalls, to demonstrate their vulnerability at times. They make mistakes but uppermost in their minds is to get the job done. There are many of them who, much more than I, did it hard all their careers. I am happy to state that recently the industrial system awarded them a decent pay rise.

Are there differences between the police nowadays and in my time? It is true that police are a reflection of our society; they can't stand apart from it. In my time, we 'policed' a community of high standards. Many people had been in the armed forces. Most were self-disciplined; their expectations were not overly high. Fathers policed their own domains in a way. As a cop, you were expected to get a result with the minimum of fuss and/or paperwork. A hell of a lot of common sense was applied. In short, the boundaries were defined and it was not hard to stick to them. Kids were strictly controlled at school. There were not too many dropouts. Any paedophiles known or seen in an area where they shouldn't be were quickly and sometimes violently removed. Society in all lived, I suppose, in a benevolent dictatorship.

The officers of today are faced with the change of goals, higher expectations, more demands. Due to litigation, they have not the freedom to apply justice too often. What you get from them is the law. No point blaming the police for the slide in moral, ethical standards. Police are still the same in their minds as they were in my day and before. With one big difference: the standards of the public have dropped considerably. But police are still required, probably more so than in my day, to maintain a standard that is far above modern society. That is a hard road to follow. Police are frustrated at not being able to tie up a job because of time constraints, and they come out looking like robots. Nobody is told to piss off, for fear of a bunch of sanctimonious do-gooders coming down on top of them. All the pay in the world won't cure it. Some leave the job as soon as they can find a spot out of the limelight. I saw it coming.

There are some wrongs in life we cannot fix. I would not attempt to heal any wounds I may have inflicted, even small ones. Cutting remarks can never be undone. I try to bury demons as I travel on my journey. If that involves more humility from me, then I readily accede to it. I read much more inspirational literature nowadays. I write a bit of it. I maintain a sense of humour but regulate the type. I can sit for long hours just listening to the sounds of nature. I walk a lot; I talk to myself while I walk. So far I have not been stopped and questioned by police. I really let the world roll by.

Bad things happen to good people. They always have and they always will. With much help from GE with his wisdom, I have learned to just be. He told me I would write another round of memoirs about my time in the police and also our connections. He is more confident than I about being published, though. He hates doubters.

Part II

'I like the silent church, before the service begins, better than the preaching.' – Ralph Waldo Emerson

10

Grey Eagle

Yes, you have guessed. He is a native American and my spiritual guide. Why Red Indians? You might have guessed that as well but in case you are not up with matters of the spirit, indigenous peoples are closer to the Earth and, as such, closer to God, and, in spite of the mouthing off by many religious folk, are really onto the existence of God. I am as well, after years of slipping in and out of beliefs. Years of switching to steadfast stuff and sliding into agnosticism (hedging my bets, some would say). I am like Carl Jung now. If asked, I just say, 'Believing is seeing.' Not the reverse.

Through this book you will find many quotes from Grey Eagle, with his wisdom shining through from beyond the veil, in that world Hamlet called 'the undiscovered country'.

It has been a long process for me, with beginnings way back, back into childhood sickness, and back into a time when children died of some of those diseases. Back to when I was solitary. Like an oyster, secret and contained, my parents were like moss growing on porous cement slabs. Silent and stable. I made my move on from Mr Solitaire with what life brings and acceptance, yet expressing gratitude for the twists and turns and the beauty which lies behind the twists.

11

Beginnings

I remember them all with clarity: the small starts, the big ones and the life-changing fearful beginnings which left in their wake a dry mouth, a tumbling whirlpool which took my whole body on a shuddering ride into a dark world and then a dazzling bright one with long fingers reaching out towards me. Moaning rasping voices accompanied a background of choirs, which blocked out the groans until I was turned around by an unseen hand and sent back in a flash to my bedroom, with my mouth throbbing with dull red pain, like a devil's toothache.

I learnt quickly to keep the happenings to myself. They left me half awake in the mornings and consequently caused a lot of heartache with some grumpy teachers. A report showed that I had no powers of concentration at times.

Sunday school fixed it, when I learnt to pray to God to keep me awake in school. I never forgot it but, like all of us, was led astray by the lure of life and all of its adventures. God was for later, I thought – for the dull people and the old. Before the prayer, before the night sweats, before the pneumonia, which sent me into another frenzied world, there was my world of the one-acre block at South Payneham with the trees, the birds and the animals next door.

Seven is the age when kids are supposed to stop talking to their angels but in my case it went on for six more years with my ghost dogs and a cow. They came and went with wagging tails and bright eyes. Their happy eyes went with me up to the ceiling. My cow went moo and pooped copious amounts as she walked along by my side (but she didn't jump over the moon). There we were, us happy three looking down at my body and the doctor with his stethoscope always around his red neck, worn like a trophy. Mum and Dad were there too, on the first night, gazing at their coughing child.

But not all of my trips up to the ceiling and beyond were unhappy, or mysterious, just tiring the next day, that's all. There were no relatives on my journey who I knew, which is explainable, as I was not aware of my adoptive status till I was forty-four years of age. Spirits apparently kept close their family secrets. That secret was revealed to me by an excellent medium who had my birth mother standing beside her, which took me on another journey of discovery.

Doctor Dunstone stood with my parents on the third night of the out of body experience (OBE) and I heard his words when I started coming down from the plaster, just missing the swinging light socket.

'It's touch and go, Ivy. Keep his temperature down. I'll call again tomorrow.'

And he did, along with sulphur tablets shoved down my prised-open mouth and with doses of Lanes milk emulsion, which caused many itches for years, until I saw Errol Harding, a naturopath, when I was twenty-four years old, who got rid of the residue basking in my kidneys (having a great time of it) with some of his pills, potions and creams.

I accepted the OBEs with some reluctance and not aware that I was chaperoned right through the business of childhood with all of its dramas. I took it as part of my life: I thought all kids had them.

*

The old gypsy woman in her colourful caravan and colourful kids, opposite in the school oval, set the record straight (until the local cops moved them on). 'Do not be scared, boy. It will all go away when you turn thirteen years of age,' she whispered, and it did.

Sunday school really helped, particularly when I was in the school choir. However, that happy episode came to a halt when I had a farting fit during practice, and from then on was banned. By the time the farting stopped, I had a racing bike and rode for miles with my friends.

Peter Rogers was run over by a truck and killed on the Mount Barker Road. His spirit came to me for many nights. 'I'm happy, Ray.' And he showed me the toys he was making. Many more spirits came and stayed for a few minutes but nothing was said. They looked OK and just went away. I took them for granted. They never worried me, apart from the freezing cold when they were nearby.

The years from fourteen to twenty were lean regarding spirits. But there were many scary life-threatening moments like motorcycle accidents. I was nearly drowned and I think now it was a near-death experience (NDE). I was revived, without any meetings or dark tunnels to cope with.

Sadly, I stopped my dialogue with God in those years and I did not meet with my guide and in fact did not know what guides were until I attended an amateur, badly conducted séance just after I came out of the navy. It was with friends and the usual fingers on a glass with the glass moving rapidly. Some laughter, some sarcasm, but the spinning glass told some truths.

One of the members was killed on his motorbike. Another one hanged himself after being sexually abused and another one was involved in a messy divorce and came off second best, with the husband bashing him senseless.

The séance with uneducated sitters was not for me any more. I have read much about that subject and they are OK if the circle is protected by fervent prayers but even then the chance of mischief developing is high.

I had skimmed through life like a swimmer who concentrates on ploughing along on the surface, never diving to investigate the world beneath, a world of another stratum filled with the life of plants, of fish, of mammals, existing side by side in an environment devoid of human beings. The skimming had to slow down. My air had been punctuated with illusion on illusion and I had to find a way to separate from the baggage: maybe God was the answer, just maybe?

12

You Can't Always Get What You Want

'My understanding of the fundamental laws of the Universe did not come out of my mind.' – Albert Einstein

The words from the Rolling Stones song have haunted me for many years. They were words to live by but, like Mick and his mates, they were quickly forgotten with a crammed life. A life of constantly seeking recognition, stuck between affiliation, according to Professor Maslow and his hierarchy of needs. My life changed after the accidental electrocution when I was around twenty-three and I floated away from the pain with my pulse stopping along a green tunnel. I was out for over six minutes until I was revived, which puts the kibosh on the opinion of scientists. They pronounce it's all from the brain, from the deprivation of oxygen, yet when we band of brothers of the 'over four minutes tribe' speak out, the medical people just dismiss it. And to this day, other men and women with great brains (in their ignorance) call it 'garbage' and all of us NDE people turn away from the scientists who believe us to be deluded or, worse, attention grabbers.

I acknowledged God right after the experience and started to read a lot of books about NDEs and OBEs, and about Buddhism, as well as sprinklings from the Bible. Those years were crammed and, according to the tenets of Buddhism, I filled my life with exercise, study, marriage, children, mortgages and all the usual stuff which people encounter. I was running around like an unregistered dog, like a mouse trapped in a tidy bin. All along, a voice whispered in my ear, 'Stop praying for wants. God will supply your needs.' But I didn't listen. I should have, because the words from the Rolling Stones were apt.

My need for affiliation was high. I was fearful that my smart-arse, joke-telling macho-man image would come crashing down in the police, which is a cauldron of mocking jokes, hard-line emotional scenes and heart-rending decisions. Dotted in amongst all those trials was always a need to maintain the image of the good guy, the warrior charging in to do battle for the good, for the triumph over evil. It is no wonder so many cops fall by the wayside. So my need to speak out openly about a love of God was constrained and stayed constrained until later in life. Cops are the best in the world for labelling people. No one within the police in those days wanted to be labelled as a God botherer.

I mouthed the words of prayers and sang hymns in my visits to spiritualist churches. Always seeking, always seeking.

Fred Souter from the Carrington Street Church in Adelaide said many times, 'You are a seeker of the truth, but it will take a long time. It's not under some rock or in a lake or a magic sword called Excalibur.' He added, 'Reading will not bring out the truth. You have guides who are shaking their heads in dismay.'

How right was all that advice, which sank in much later? In that charged atmosphere within the church, a thought occurred to me. Was I like Peter, who denounced Jesus, along with the others, denying that he ever knew him? Was I just a hollow man? I certainly felt I was and my path was not getting any clearer.

My then-wife remarked, 'You've got to stop reading all that stuff. I'm scared of what you might bring into this house,' but I dismissed her fears.

She was right but I missed the point for years and, as they say, I fell off the perch once the marriage broke up years later, realising I had missed the messages which came my way.

All those synchronicities. All those signs. All those symbols, none of which jarred my waking mind. That is, until I watched Stella Derwood on Channel Nine talking about her psychic abilities and couldn't wait till Sunday. But she wasn't there. It would have to wait.

Meanwhile, I had some dreams which kept telling me about secrets. I was back in the garden of my childhood, observing birds and the patterns of the clouds in the dream. I wondered at the odd fact that I could observe, losing myself, merging into the landscape, yet still be alert enough to notice other occurrences and take notes. In one dream, I shouted to a very old man that I was made of two parts: the main body that lives it all, all the history behind and more to follow with all of its pain, joy and the mundane; and the observer part that is like a silent sentinel without emotion yet is able to kick start the main body just like a security guard who stands motionless, ready to act in a crisis.

I shouted to the old man, 'The sentinel is the real me who controls it all. That is not the one I see in the mirror but I know now it is me. Nothing can ever hurt me.'

The old man with the long beard suddenly grew and I am sure he was either God or someone very close to him. He smiled at me in the dream and that image has never left me.

13

Family Secrets

'Divine guidance often comes when the horizon is the blackest.' –
Mahatma Gandhi

My dreams were explicit and I decided I would consult a medium. Her name was Jessie and from the outset she spoke about the process, though I guessed she sensed some of my knowledge of such matters.

I listened without interrupting. This is what she told me. She saw uniforms all around me. Blood was everywhere. My mother was sending a message for me to seek the truth. (But Mum was still alive. What's this about, I thought.) The spirit of the lady was described as five foot four inches, slender with bright green eyes and long auburn hair across her shoulders. A strong cleft chin, which I have. She died when she was twenty-five years of age in a northern hospital with a lung infection when I was around eighteen months old. I had been born in Osmond Terrace, Norwood. My mother's name was Lil or Phil; her husband's name also had an L. I was given to her best friends Harry and Ivy Clift sometime after she died. I was to be told when I was twenty-one but it had not occurred. Her parents were in spirit with her. Her father was once an SA cop.

Jessie came out of her trance state and we shook hands. I left completely puzzled. I felt the urge to follow it up, but never asked Mum, because she must have had a reason for her silence all of those years.

As the result of phone calls and some serendipity, I found that I was born Raymond John Lang. My birth father was Lindsay Gordon Lang and he was still alive in Naracoorte with many kids. My birth mother's name was Phyllis May Lawrence. Her younger sister Doris Manser described her exactly as the medium had said and showed me some photos which fitted as well. Phyllis died of TB in the Northfield infectious disease hospital, and the Lawrence family (whose father had been a cop and suffered after watching an execution) never forgave Lang for his alleged neglect. Peter Lang, my actual uncle, was my senior man in the police but we never knew about our connection back then. Dave Harris, a former mate from the police, was married to a sister-in-law of Lindsay Lang, the youngest of the Lang family. His mother Mary nursed Phyllis in the Northfield infectious diseases hospital until she died of consumption. Rhonda Lamb (née Lawrence) was my cousin and was the mother of Debra Lamb, one of the Truro murder victims. Rhonda never got over it and died quite young. As did her husband Ray, who I knew from the Army Reserve. A girl who was murdered on a western suburbs beach was a sister-in-law to Danny Lang, one of the Lang boys, my half-brother.

So you think there is nothing out there. However, with regard to connections, there is more.

My birth grandmother was a Barrett. A good friend from the police was Chris Sharp. His sister Margaret married Brian Stratman. Brian Stratman's uncle married a Barrett who turned about to be a close relative of mine. Ken Gluche was a lawyer and a former SA cop who I knew well and whose parents were best friends with Brian Stratman. KG was a cousin to Julie Cox who married Ron Lang, one of my half-brothers.

Maybe we are all related down the track. It sounds a bit like an old 1950s song called 'I'm my own Grandpa'.

14

Stella and Len Darwood

For me, Stella and Len were the best thing since sliced bread. With their vast knowledge, they gave credence to all the material I had read for fifteen years. She was an attractive woman in her middle age with bright gleaming bold eyes which shone out from her glasses. Len and she were World War II veterans. She was with the Royal Navy and Len was a Royal Marine warrant officer who had seen much action and wondered where we go to after death. Stella had always been clairvoyant and saw spirits. Len was more intuitive. I learnt much from them and joined Stella's development circle. I saw spirits in the darkened room and heard some amazing evidence from the etheric world.

Hand healing was taught and for a time I was proficient at it but after Stella's death I lost interest. She was my earthly guide and it was she who told me about my guide and named him Grey Eagle. Did I actually see him in those days? Yes, for a brief flash, and I dreamed of him. However, love and the business of life took hold after her early death, which was followed by a huge funeral crowded with most of the spiritualist fraternity.

Sadly, two days before her passing, she thought that God had deserted her and ruefully said to me, 'After all I've done to help others!'

It was a tearful episode with her wasted body, due to a virulent stomach cancer. Apart from holding her hand, there was nothing I, or Todd my boss at the time and also interested in spiritual matters, could do except just pray silently. I walked out to the car and knew the next time I would see her would be at her funeral.

The weather was mild but I felt cold and my hands were clammy. The itch started on the back of my head. I sat for a while thinking about her and adjusted the rear-vision mirror; in that flash I saw Grey Eagle sitting in the back.

'Someone walk over your grave, Raymond?'

I did not look in the mirror. I wanted him to stay, so I spoke. 'When, Grey Eagle, when will she pass?'

'Two days, Raymond. Don't worry: she will rest for a long time until she gets over this.'

I thought on his words and started the car and once again GE spoke.

'Len will be very ill soon with diabetes. His legs will be amputated.'

Bloody hell, I thought, as I drove off with memories flooding my head. The trance state Stella put me in one night at her circle flashed back. I had a mild OBE but I could see the people in the group in the room, with only a red light. I spoke, but my voice seemed far away. I felt fire on my hands and saw I was in a cockpit in a fighter plane and looked at a date scrawled on paper inside the cockpit. It was August 1940 and I was in the Battle of Britain and my plane was on fire. The canopy was jammed and I screamed but then I saw that it was not me. It was a young man wearing an RAF uniform with one blue ring on the sleeve. He banged on the canopy but it would not open and then there was a splash when he hit the ocean. I saw his spirit rise and he stood speaking to me.

'I am George Butterworth.' He pointed to a member of the group.

After I came back to consciousness, the woman about Stella's age who he pointed at said, 'I'll have to check this out but I think he is related.'

I never followed it up because the group closed sometime later.

That was the last time I went into a deep trance state and I shivered for days after with a unbearable cold which came with attacks of the 'runs' to the toilet.

*

Stella's funeral came and went, as did Len's some months later, and I realised my two mentors had gone. What knowledge had they had and what sights had they seen in their lives within the London spiritualist movement? They saw tables rising, spirits materialising before their eyes, some speaking in foreign languages and placing healing hands on the sitters. Such was the power of the circles and the trance mediums in those days. And they knew them all: Helen Duncan and Mr Flint; Sir Oliver Lodge came through as well on a sitting, along with members of the murdered Tsar of Russia with his family. Apports were produced and handled and a woman was left with a precious gemstone which remained with her. Stella and Len emigrated later on. Remarkable healing was carried out on some, and a woman who suffered badly with polio and wore calipers chucked away her leg irons.

I gave up on my wanderings and journeys into the veil beyond in 1982, the year of my divorce, and just got on with building another house and helping my children. As well, the Army Reserve beckoned again, which I just dismissed. Stella said she saw me in a green uniform and she also predicted the wars in the Middle East would break out, much more towards the end of the century.

Six Years Before

My great dad died suddenly and Mum came to live with us. Dad was there in spirit many times. I saw him in the kitchen, in the bathroom and sitting on Mum's bed. I tried to speak to him but I did not get a reply. My two daughters saw him as well. Kerry woke up with him sitting on her bed one night. Joanne (Jo) experienced him just after we bought a cat she named Candy, who tore off into a corner when Jo spoke to Dad. Stella thought he had gone onto another better plane.

So ghosts were always around me. And more were to come. GE warned me in a dream and with some writing as well.

GE: Do not make any hasty decisions concerning your wife Marlene.

Me: But she has left. She's to be married again next year.

GE: There is a chance that may not happen. Leave her be. Do not worry her and leave the relationship you are in. It is not good for you.

Me: Hey, where were you when all this happened? I was lonely.

GE: I told you before, I can't always fix relationships. I can just give warnings. You have free will from God, you know.

However, I did not take his advice and for some years I became insular, just drifting as if all the great stuff I had read, embraced and preached about was all for nothing. GE and I did not speak for some time.

15

1985

Mum's spirit came back to me two days after she died in her pensioner flat at Marden. She was as visible to me as a piece of coal lying in snow. Her expression was not one of happiness because I think she had not found her beloved Harry at this point and he was the love of her life. I was busy at the kitchen sink after having removed some money from under her mattress (she had often told me to search there and being a child of the Depression she was anxious that it be passed on). I wondered if she was angry about her dog Rusty, who was old and frail and could not join her in her flat. We had to find other ways for him to go and we did. It occurred to me that she was angry about my search for birth parents just to discover roots. It did not worry me. However, I believe it played on her mind. I never spotted her spirit from that day. Yet Dad came a few times, smiled and whisked away into the night, with nary a scent of his presence.

It was time to restart my search and I did. I found the small church at Northfield effectively managed by Sheila Castle and it helped to ease my way in because her husband Dennis was a former SA cop who I worked with. I attended regularly and for many years heard many stage clairvoyants giving out messages and many of those messages came to pass in the fullness of time. I still attend when I can, if only to absorb the atmosphere.

1991

I was by then out of the SA police at age fifty-five years and had joined the sheriff's office as a court orderly. Another career came on which lasted for fifteen years, embroiling me with another circle of friends and acquaintances, many of whom I read tarot cards for. The most significant card reading came to me after I tired of my wood-turning hobby of five years. I mean, how many wooden bowls can one turn for friends, until they either draw their blinds when they see you coming with another bowl, or you see it sitting in the backyard as a dog's food container?

The six of cups came up three times and spoke to me. 'Return to an old skill,' they yelled. I thought about it and after a dream I knew it would be writing, which was the oldest skill, and that was when the handwritten notes started, along with a dream diary covered with the stain of white wine spillages when I wrote into the early hours. Sometimes I shouted in joy when the words formed, or swore when nothing happened. The old writer's block hits every writer. The famous music was retained from back in my life, even though I thought it had left me. The disco beat thumped away in my head along with Abba, who sang their life with all its ups and downs, and in their words I found the ability to cope with the ups and downs which all families have. I found joy in all of the music, which I am sure cured me from my drift into melancholy; some of it entered into later manuscripts. I was not aware of what part music would play once I started to write in earnest, but that was predicted by mediums for the next decade.

Much later I was asked after a book launch, 'Where do you get your quirky sayings from?'

Quirky, I thought? I paused for a while because the question needed a straight answer.

'I immerse myself in my five senses, which is nothing to do with luck and nothing to do with thoughts, because we need to think a bit less and feel a bit more. Above all, trust the feelings. The writing then comes.'

The questioner nodded while I gazed straight at him and said, 'But it all comes from God,' which is something I would never once have said to a stranger or even a friend.

He smiled at me, shook my hand and walked away. I knew then that my courage in speaking out had emerged. It was set in concrete forever; the concrete had fissures in it which allowed words from the heart to flow out.

16

About Prayer

'For most of your life you've lived as the effect of your experiences. Now you are invited to be the cause of them.' – Neal Donald Walsch

Let's get this straight: I pray to God but I talk to guides and angels (in meditation at times). My guide Grey Eagle, whose name was revealed to me by Stella Derwood, is, like most guides, not far away. It must be frustrating to them when we don't listen and I guess they either block their ears or go for a stroll – a stroll which might take years because time is of no concern to them. However, when called upon, Grey Eagle is there in a flash. No, I don't see him much, but I feel him. It is like a whiff of a summer breeze and the smell is a mixture of magnolia, wisteria and buffalo hide.

Sceptics might say, 'No, not another Indian.' However, I really don't care what they think and I take no notice of them. Ignorance is bliss for them as well as for me. Yet this I know: the senses of the guides are heightened hundreds of times more than ours. I think sceptics are like Italian gardens – all laid out in straight lines, no curves, no deviations. We are all vibrations and energy and they have to match with ours. Don't ask me how. I have never enquired. It is enough to just read the answers, with GE guiding the pen in my automatic writing sessions, and the proof is in the pudding with the several books which have been published by Ginninderra Press. It is not exactly the easiest of the arts to crack. It's like trying to row a boat when you have forgotten to release the wharf rope.

If I come back in another life and have a choice, it will be music, not writing. Sometimes I wish I had an Aboriginal guide because I would be able to smell the gum leaves and the wattle. Not that I dislike magnolia and wisteria; it is just that I am true blue and he is probably reading this while I write and maybe thinking 'ungrateful sod' or 'look what I have done for him'. Sorry, Grey Eagle – nothing personal. As to our black people, it's just that Mum had an affinity with them: she grew up in Norwood with some of the original people of the Adelaide plains.

Bill Owen and his wife came to our place a few times. Their son Mallee was killed on a motorbike when riding with my Uncle Jack, and Mum felt the sadness. Later, in my sheriff's officer role, I told Matthew Petrie, an Aboriginal legal rights lawyer, about the connection, and a week later I met Cliffy Owen, their relative and a youth worker, and he confirmed the connections with my mum. It was 1999 and I wished she was there to hear that bit of confirmation from her past. Maybe Mum would have come through to me if I had an Aboriginal guide. (Please don't be put out about this, GE.)

Dreams in bright colours came into my life for at least a month after the message from the tarot cards. I was sitting by a pretty lake and GE was there with his full headdress, not looking in my direction but just gazing at the aqua-blue lake. We each threw pebbles into the lake and I knew he was waiting for my questions. The big one came out about prayer but his answer was short and concise. It was delivered in a deep baritone voice with no trace of an accent.

'You can't ask for anything in prayer, because God already knows your innermost thoughts. But not your wants – they are another matter. A prohibited matter. It is the needs which he concerns himself with, so we should not pray for other things, but should ask for more of God.'

I just sat there taking it all in yet thinking about Mick Jagger and his song.

'Do you think I am a mirage, Raymond? A lot of people might think that is what you see.'

'Of course not. Grey Eagle.'

'I've been there all along, you know. I was there when you crawled over the ceiling when you were ill and it was me who bought you back.'

I stammered, 'Like you have been there all my life. All my mistakes.' I flushed with embarrassment when I remembered the farts in the choir.

He read my mind. 'Your queen farts. So what? Preachers fart but they are silent ones in the pulpit. God laughs as well.'

I did not speak as I was still red. I saw my red face reflected in the lake and chucked a pebble in to break up the reflection.

'I was there when you were pushed to the bottom of the pool and had what you humans call an NDE and I was there when that man took a shot at you in the city.-I was there when you were electrocuted and were on the way to heaven. I took you back. I was there when you took the rifle off the man later and also had a big hepatitis A injection after, as did the two girls, and I saw them wince in pain.'

I thought to myself, bloody hell, this guide knows everything from the moment of my birth to now, every bloody second. I thought for a long minute, which was probably more like a bleep, while I was lost in what to say next but I came up with a question. 'What about the man with the shotgun?'

'Yes, that too.'

The staggering news caused a stomach rumble and for a while I felt I might faint. Yet I recovered. 'Is it boring for you? I mean, do you have anyone else to take care of?'

'Yes, it can be tiring.'

'Do guides sleep?' Which was followed with 'Were you ever missing from my life?'

'No, but sometimes I wish I had been. You were driven by your ego a lot, you know. But there is one thing I would like you to stop.'

'What is it?'

'Stop imitating John Wayne. Us Indians are sick of him.'

Once again, I was embarrassed, yet a bit amused as well. I nodded again about the ego stuff. I knew what he meant. But it was too painful to speak about.

The dream concluded but many more were to come before the automatic writing started. On that occasion we just sat still and silent, chucking pebbles in the lake and listening for the sound of the splash and watching the gentle ripples. I woke with two pebbles on my bed, which confirmed a bit more in the way of evidence. I had read much about apports and Stella hold told me about what she had seen. I picked them up and watched them fade away in my hands. It was revealing for me because I started to pray with some conviction and sending out grace, grateful for my life.

17

Ghostly Business

'And whenever you pray, do not be like the hypocrites: they love to stand and pray at the synagogue and at street corners, so that they may be seen by others. Truly I tell you they have received their reward but when you pray, go into your room and shut the door and pray to your father in secret and your father who sees you in secret will reward you.'
– Matthew 6:56

My three decades of research had sustained an objective approach with regard to earthbound spirits and I was not being put off because of fear of the unknown, unlike most people who fear it – and naturally so with the vast amount of propaganda thrust down our throats, with scary films, scary books and preachers abounding, spruiking the end of the world, all yelling out, 'Jesus will save you, Jesus will save you.' What about the people who had not had the privilege to meet him?

I understood the signs which indicated the presence of a spirit, which led me on journeys with the usual précis of how, what, where after meeting the apparition, or at least feeling its presence. Several times, my memory is aided with small jotted notes which are essential to ensure that the story comes out with a ring of truth. I keep the mind aside from the memory. One is for the soul, the other is for the brain.

Carol is my cousin, the daughter of Auntie Doris Manser, whose help with my 1977 jigsaw with regard to my family secrets was invaluable. Carol and Brian (her then-husband) were Australian air force personnel who lived near the RAAF base at Edinburgh in Adelaide's northern suburbs. They were often woken from a deep sleep with the loud metallic noise of a clump on their roof, which was followed by another slamming sound on metal and a sound of boots stomping on metal. It was too much to bear and it kept their two young daughters awake some nights. They were fearful about speaking out because of jeers and laughter. They were well aware of my interest in such matters and called on my services. I obliged and attended late one night to witness the strange events. I was not disappointed with what I heard, because it was exactly as she said. There they were, the crashing sounds. Something had to be done. We checked outside by torchlight, but no signs of human intervention were obvious. Something supernatural was at work. We both made enquiries, separately, just like two mountain climbers ascending a face from opposite sides, yet reaching the summit simultaneously. Our notes were identical.

During World War II, the area was devoid of housing because it was a tank training area. The noises we heard were of tanks stopping, reversing, turrets turning, a crew climbing up and down with their heavy boots on the sides of the tank and slamming the lid down during the training. Army records revealed there were some deaths due to accidents and suicides: it was reasonable to assume some of those men were still stuck on Earth.

I called in Stella and Len and their crew, who went through the house with our friendly priest, spreading holy water, saying prayers and burning sage in the corners. The troubled souls must have moved on towards the light and my cousin was relieved. As were Stella, Len and the group.

My friends Brian and Carol Knowles were believers. I thought then that they were extremely open-minded, embracing many New Age ideas despite Brian having been a detective sergeant, hard-nosed and forthright, who had watched many violent scenes played out in his profession, and talked them over in his chats with me. And he knew my views, which caused him to call for help to understand why his deceased mother-in-law's rocking chair was always rocking at the same time each night and caused their two German shepherds to charge outside in fear. There they huddled regardless of the weather outside away from the sounds of the vacant chair, SQUEAK, THUD, SQUEAK, THUD, SQUEAK, THUD, with their fearful eyes darting about. It certainly was a bit scary. I stood watching the chair with my usual signs circling around. My scalp was itchy, my torso rumbled and the dry mouth was prominent; I knew she was there in the chair, in the freezing cold, on a warm night. We three stood holding hands and chanting the Lord's Prayer with loud voices till the chair slowed. Their mother had been a practising Catholic, so after a joint discussion, a priest came along a few days later and spread holy water about the place.

Brian chopped up the chair after the presence had gone. 'It's not that we disapproved of her – after all, we loved her – but it was causing bedlam with the dogs and the neighbours and Mum had to go to the light instead of being stuck here all day, Ray.'

I agreed with him.

Gerry was one of my speed cops, based at Para Hill patrol base. To say that he was a busy man is an understatement. He owned an earthmoving business and the moonlighting topped up his income. In spite of the rank difference, we got on well because he was a laugh a minute and did not take himself too seriously, which I believe is an essential ingredient for all people to survive in the world without too much in the way of hang-ups later in life. Gerry knew my views and had an open mind and I was the one he turned to just after he and Debbie purchased the old 1840s-era house in Willaston, just out of Gawler. It had been an old hotel and in its heyday was a stopover for people rushing to the goldfields of Ballarat.

Debbie and her baby were woken many nights by the sounds of scratching followed by moans. Gerry, always the busy man, was restoring the old walls and uncovering old newspapers of the day; he thought the sounds came from possums or maybe rats inside the cavities. Pest exterminators found nothing and Gerry looked for something else – something from another place.

Debbie woke up shrieking one night; she had had a bad dream of a man sitting on her bed. She made a cup of tea and spoke to Gerry about it and went back to bed. Gerry, who had resigned after a few bosses thought he ought to devote all of his efforts to SAPOL, was off early in the morning with his tasks.

Debbie brushed her hair in the morning and looked again in the mirror. Sitting on the bed was the man out of her dreams. She closed her eyes and opened them. He was still there in his frock coat with the red lapels and the knee-length boots with the tops turned over revealing tan kid-glove leather. She did not flee this time but just took the baby to another room and busied herself all day until Gerry arrived home, when she presented him with the facts of the vision in their bedroom. Gerry walked in and looked at the bed and saw an impression sunk into the bedspread, larger than small Debbie, and he called on me.

I called the next night and spoke to them both. The closer I got to the room, the colder it got and the scalp, the tummy and the dry throat came upon me. I turned around at the sound of a muffled cough but no one was there. I believed their story.

Debbie added, 'His eyes were not angry, I know that…just confused – but what's he doing here?'

'Might be a sudden death one way or another. Remember, this was a hotel. Could have been many deaths which we'll probably never find out about. Too late for anyone living around here to know who he was.'

They both stared at each other.

Gerry spoke. 'People around here know the place is haunted. That's why it sat unoccupied for years.'

'Best get a priest to come here, I reckon, and bless the place. I had some luck recently with Bugsy – you know, Brian Knowles. I'll get onto him.' Which I did, and the ghost never came back.

Gerry and Debbie eventually sold their house. After buying a prawn boat, Gerry became a millionaire in Queensland. So much for the bosses in SAPOL who couldn't wait to get rid of him. He just didn't fit their profile. Probably a bit too laconic. Like me.

Rick Pearson was the licensee of the Murray Street Gawler Hotel for a time after he left the CIB at Holden Hill. I knew Rick well. He was an intelligent likeable fellow who I knew would do well in the hotel with another mate from SAPOL who had resigned as well. He was aware of my interest in the unknown and called on me. I took my daughter Jo with me. Jo is proficient at automatic writing and a stubborn Taurus, not easily put off or fooled. She heard, smelt and sometimes saw spirits and I think that so-called gift has come down to my grandchildren (Elise, Matthew and Benjamin), who saw angels as a kid. It is also on her mother's side – the Sims, with dear old Auntie Ev, who was magic incarnated and a visionary woman.

'It's been here for some time, Ray, in one of the upstairs bedrooms. The rumour is someone killed himself,' Rick told us.

Jo prowled about the room until the door slammed on her and she banged on it furiously. I opened it and we stood silently in the room while she lowered her head and breathed deeply. She was still for some time and yet I felt nothing eventually realising that the presence was concentrating on Jo and not me.

Jo smiled and nodded as if she was having a conversation. She stopped and said, 'Let's walk out into the passage, Dad.'

'OK, Jo,' I said. 'What did you get? Is it a woman?'

'This I know: she's stuck here and doesn't know where she is. I think she lost a baby by miscarriage or whatever.'

We said a silent prayer and explained to Rick what had happened.

'Actually, we don't really mind. It seems to be harmless but the cleaners won't go in the room. I know it adds a bit of colour to the place and maybe more customers.'

'Do you need a priest to bless the place?'

'Nah. Let it go. Just wanted to sew up the loose ends really.'

'Once a cop, always one, Rick. '

'Isn't that the truth, Ray,' he said.

Sadly years later, after Rick had sold out, he was tragically killed in a car accident at Templar's, well away from Gawler. I hope his spirit is not stuck.

Kerry, my oldest daughter, has gifts different from her younger sister's. They are highly intuitive with their five senses, which can be a curse at times, particularly if, due to sickness or lack of sleep, the aura becomes unsealed, which allows for the passing emotions of strangers to be visited on her, though she well knows how to seal her aura and does the exercise frequently. She had to learn the sealing process very quickly once she began work in the social work field, which involves being an unwilling sponge to the less fortunate clients, many of them in a drug-addicted state and quite a few more bordering on madness. Couple this with some decadence from the clients, some envy (the you've-got-it, why-shouldn't-I-have-it way of looking at life) and the trauma of sexual abuse which many have endured, and you get a violent toxic cocktail which is bound at times to snag one's anchor chain. Once snagged, it's hard to unsnag. Yet the job has its rewards as well, insofar as she has put a lot of people back on the track; therein lies the satisfaction. A darker side to her world is that when that venom is released into the atmosphere it attaches its energy onto earthbound spirits, some of whom were nasty, evil and insane in their earthly life and are still nasty and evil (not insane over there) and look to upset normal people in their times of stress. Turning a mirror back towards those who might be trying to send harm out is useful, but one needs to know who that is for it to work.

Of course, this phenomenon is not exclusive to social workers. It extends to correctional services staff, some sections of the police (particularly drug enforcement, who need to keep a careful watch on distancing themselves when off duty) and, I imagine, some defence people fighting in countries against people well able to send out horror on the airwaves by just preaching malignant hatred in the form of mantras to a long-dead relative who can send it back via energy to the earth.

Kerry has been brushed by some bad spirits, yet she was able to ward them off with her collection of the right gear: gemstones, Celtic crosses, lots of garlic, good books such as Dion Fortune used to put out, and sharing her fears with close friends. Getting it off her chest is a sure-fire way to help, especially for Gemini folk. Yet all of those aids didn't stop the nightly visit of a smell, dense atmosphere, the sound of clothes being shucked off and a big dark shape holding her down in her Walkerville flat, trying to pull her bedclothes off. One tried to strangle her. She pulled the doona over her head because of the unusual cold, the now-rotten smell and groping cold fingers, and prayed earnestly to Jesus for help. I am told he uses many sources to help those in peril and it helped for a few hours. She knew a Baptist minister, Russ B, who was a bit alternative. He gave her a Velcro cross and a great picture of Jesus which stayed over her bed from that time on.

She had had enough and I could see her demeanour was slipping. She was not the bright-eyed intelligent girl at that stage of her life. Her nights of terror went on and probably attached themselves (we think there were two taking it in turns) to the new tenants after she packed up and took the two icons with her when she moved to Marryatville to get as far away from Walkerville as possible. More dark shadows came but I suspect they were different.

There were other freaky things which occurred over the years but I believe nowadays she wards them off with a quick flick of her fingers, maybe using the tough jargon of the world we know: 'Piss off, you're not wanted.' However, her senses still tell her when the phone will ring and who will be on the other end. (The same happens with Jo and me on occasions.)

A few years back, she dreamt about Billy Thorpe our rock icon and was told he had died. She told her flatmate that night. She was making toast when the announcement of his death the night before came on the radio, which caused her to drop her toast and sit down. Her flatmate was very scared about what she had seen in the dream. It is, after all, a bit scary. She had vivid dreams about Andrew (her husband) before she met him. She was concerned about a man up the road. It all came to pass. However, she did not meet him in the nearby street. She met him at the Ingle Farm shops, where she worked as a counsellor. Her firm had a section which found jobs for unemployed people and he had come in for a session in order to find employment.

Yet I am not surprised because many years ago her mother visited Rosemary, a well known medium at Black Forest, who told her that Kerry would not meet the love of her life till she was in her mid-forties, that he had a young son, that he was from overseas and a very handy man, and that Kerry would have a series of life-threatening operations. Andrew Cox is a very handy man, now in social work as well, and is a New Zealander.

I could fill another book with many other accurate readings I have heard, as well as the not so good ones. However, it does not pay to lead a life based on what the stars say each day, or what a tarot reader might pick up, or a medium.

Stella explained about readings quite simply to me some time ago. 'The medium might see a man walking along and walking under a ladder and a paint tin is about to fall. But the painter grabs the tin and stops it and falls at the same time, missing the unsuspecting walker. It is the little grab which she does not see.'

And it is the little grabs in life which we ignore. We must watch for them and analyse them. Some may be just trivial but many are signs which we can act on. Our daily lives are full of meanings if we latch onto them. The now is most important and an Eskimo saying is appropriate: 'Yesterday is ashes, tomorrow is wood. Only today does the fire burn bright.'

Percy and Mary Broadhead lived at Gilles Plains, within stone throwing distance of the very large Holden Hill police base where I served with my friend Chris Sharp. They came to Australia during the burgeoning years after the war when the pollies preached 'populate or die'. (Which was a rather stupid slogan and ought to be in the box which also contains the 'yellow peril 'and the 'Reds are almost under the bed'. If they had been under my grandparents' bed, all they would have found was a chamber pot.)

Percy and Mary were friends of Chris for many years and I enjoyed their company, their talks and their hospitality. Percy was a nuggety, tough sort of bloke who could speak on most subjects. He was a Royal Navy submariner during the war merely because it paid more money. Some of the stories he told were certainly not in the rousing *Cruel Sea* mode with everyone doing their duty happily without grumbles. The most memorable story he told was being on duty and woken up from his hammock, which someone else then occupied. And so it went on. Imagine one after the other in a closeted hammock containing all the flakes of skin which the body sheds, drops of urine also, and, far worse, the residue left over after nocturnal emissions from the young teenage sailors. Not something we care to think about.

So that was Percy: frank and yet cheerful on the occasions I met him. Chris must have told him about my interest in the supernatural because he related a narrative about his experience in an old house in England before the rush to Australia. 'Ghost story, Ray. I'll tell you one with a happy ending. It involves music.'

I loved listening to stories of music and phantom orchestras playing 'Stella by Starlight' type tunes like the old Ray Milland movie called *The Uninvited*, in which a phantom embittered wife possessed her husband. She was like a dog with two bones; she had affairs yet wanted him around, under her elbow, and didn't approve of his new woman. It was on my mind until the story moved on, with the narrator Percy giving us little titbits, and then I knew this was no romance because his story had none of the romance of a Barbara Taylor Bradford novel. It was more like a Simpsons TV script with a quick-fix cure.

The house was a two-storey affair with a winding staircase and portraits adorning the wall all the way up, straight, evenly spaced and viewable. However, the ghost or ghosts of the house may not have liked the portraits because on most mornings the pictures were turned at crazy angles upside down towards the wall. In no time, Percy was getting sick of straightening up the hated portraits. But worse was yet to come with the piano, which played most nights – very badly, he added, and no one at the keys as they watched them depressed by some invisible force. Percy the no-nonsense man had enough of straightening up pictures and listening to badly played tunes and resolved to fix it. He did, quite radically, though it took some time.

He hand-dug a huge hole in the backyard after measuring the length, breadth and depth of the piano, which he dragged out with some effort and levered into the giant hole. In order to ensure that the ghost could not play with tons of dirt on the keys, he methodically broke the strings. And with each severing he found a tune. He was happy when he buried the piano. (He giggled in the telling of the story, as I did.) In his last act of victory, Percy grabbed all the pictures off the wall, broke them up with more giggles and sailor swear words and in they went, to befriend the remnants of the old piano. And that was the last time they heard Mozart being played badly.

Nowadays, Percy would be called a lateral thinker if he were alive. I prefer to call him a positive man who met challenges and defeated them – with some expense, however, to the management. The excavators who were engaged to build new houses decades later would have wondered how a piano got in that hole. It is a story worth telling.

*

The Chris Sharp family has ghost stories as well. After all, England is the home of ghosts; combined with India, it is a magic cauldron. Chris's parents came to Australia for the first time in 1924 and fell in love with the country. The money for the one-way trip came from an elderly relative. In order to return to catch up with relatives, the only chance they had was to save, which must have been difficult in 1930 due to the Great Depression. However, they did return and within short space of time were eager to come back to the sunshine of Australia.

There was a close Auntie Rose who lived in India for some time with her 'galloping major' husband. Her favourite pastime was the spiritualist movement, which back then was able to produce many visual phenomena.

Along with all the traditional trappings of the séances were the eager sitters waiting to have their questions asked, and hopefully to feel the warm hands materialising at times in the darkened room, with only a red light showing the way. Auntie Rose believed in God and insisted on prayers before each séance. Prayers to God to protect them from anything evil. This by all accounts worked.

The sitters arrived and included in the group was Chris's mother Cath. The room was cleared with certain rituals and the chairs were put in place, along with the red light. The sitters were required to join hands and recite the Lord's Prayer. If they didn't agree, they were promptly sent on their way. Thus, like souls were all seated in accordance with Auntie Rose and her rules. They were urged to breathe deeply beforehand, to put them into a receptive state. Then it started, with the pointer moving slowly at first and lobbing alongside who was chosen to ask a question first. The sitters were amazed with the accuracy. Cathy sat a trifle nervous and fearing when her turn would come to ask a question. She was stuck till Rose spoke.

'What is your innermost hope?'

Cathy thought about it and knew straight away. 'When will I return to Australia?'

The pointer immediately spelled out 'fifteen years'. She tried again but it still gave the same answer, which sent her into a depression.

'That can't be right,' she pronounced, but once again the same answer was given. She left, still with the despair of waiting that long in the cold of England's winters.

Yet life rolled on for the young couple and before long Margaret was born and later on in 1936 Chris emerged from the womb. The dogs of war loomed and three years later World War II broke into the life of the world and they were stuck until a chance came to move back to the land of their choice

The family embarked from Southampton on the *Strathmore* in 1946, which was exactly fifteen years later after the spirit had spoken three times. No doubt the sceptics always ready with off-the-top-of-the-head answers will try to negate it, even suggesting that Rose the leader had advance knowledge. If she did, then she had more power than the rest of the great minds in those days.

18

Possession

'I did not say it was possible. I said it happened.' – Sir William Crooks, a leader in the nineteenth century into psychic research

I have pondered often as a writer of fiction whether it's possible for a writer to become obsessed with the characters he creates within his imagination. In my case at age seventy-two I started out and within four years had written about twenty-three novellas, countless poems, many short stories and so far one unpublished novel of 70,000 words. Several novellas are on the GP website and as well I am in many anthologies of poetry and short stories.

I was on a roll with time on my hands and the ideas came in thick and fast with forty-seven years of law enforcement and the courts, fifteen years of Reserve force service mainly in Army Intelligence, meeting soldiers from our friendly forces and attending many war games. That aside, there were my decades of investigating matters of the psychic, study of law books, landscaping with native plants and passing exams which included psychology, human behaviour, the resource structure of Australia, history of Australia and Europe and the US, all without the use of glasses. I enjoyed it all with a thirst for knowledge, which has never waned. The pit of stories was bottomless yet all of the huge mixture sent my dreams for a time into a complicated flooding stream. I was stuck on a rock on a waterfall many times in my dreams and could not negotiate to a bank or even over the waterfall.

I believe it would be possible to enter into the soul of a strong created character who is the alter ego of the writer, whereby given time, the character takes over as the ventriloquist and the writer becomes the dummy. Then and only then does the dummy become surplus to needs. The character in the book or indeed the book takes over the soul. Patricia Highsmith, the author of *Strangers on a Train*, certainly thought it was possible, which takes me back forty-eight years ago to the eastern suburbs.

I was tasked to attend an old house with an outside work room. The house was owned by an old lady who had no relatives. She was a writer of many fiction stories published over the years by magazines. A housekeeper attended about once a week and saw the old lady was slipping into decline but there was no one to tell. No one else came to the house except a gardener.

She was always at her old Remington all day and most nights and was bound to end up very sick, which happened when the housekeeper found her unconscious. She died a few days later in the Royal Adelaide Hospital. A coroner's report was submitted by others but my sergeant asked that I check the letter box for any sign of letters which might reveal a relative. There was nothing there but I saw the old Remington and the hundreds of books on the shelves. The funeral notice came in the papers and out of curiosity I rode past on the station motorcycle outfit and saw people dressed in black prowling around the garden and chucking books in the old incinerator after the funeral. I enquired who they were and they produced evidence that they were the inheritors of the property – hence the book burning. I told the sergeant about the people almost jumping on her coffin but there was nothing we could do. Particularly about the burning of her treasured books. Why couldn't they wait? But that is human nature, the bad side, isn't it?

The Hillcrest Ghost

Garth and Sharon lived with us for a time at Hope Valley. We had for many years known their parents, who lived in Tasmania. Unemployment spread its depressing blanket over much of Australia, which caused the young couple to search further on the mainland. Garth was a fine strong man, a bricklayer, but the building industry was spasmodic and required hours waiting by a phone for a job to appear. Sharon, a hairdresser, was not able to find work. Conversation was light-hearted until they found out about my interest in the supernatural, which created a bond between them and me.

They read many of my books on the subject. They were from an island originally settled with convict labour and there was always the prospect of encountering many of the indigenous people slaughtered by a culture which failed to recognise the gifts and the quirks of the original black people. Yet apart from a brush past by a long-dead relative, or a wispy smell in a room of cigar smoke, their actual visual encounters were non-existent. Still they kept an open mind, connected by a thread of possibility.

However, their views changed from possibility to downright belief when they both saw a ghost, full on, standing and pointing a finger. Blazing brown eyes threatened their very existence, their right to be in the flat at Hillcrest, a neighbouring suburb, not far from Hope Valley.

John the landlord, a widower, was happy to rent the flat out to such a fine young couple and shared a few drinks with them while they settled in. His visits were regular, especially on rent money days.

Six months had gone and jobs had come their way and on most nights they flopped on the big bed and slept deep dreamless sleeps. Then it came, quiet at first with a gentle woman's voice singing World War II songs. The music seemed to come from within the walls but stopped when Garth banged on the walls. The music ceased abruptly when Sharon placed a painting of Jesus on the wall above their bed. They thought no more about it, being down to earth people and guessing a ghost or two, or even a noisy animal. But Garth struggled with Sharon's suggestion, adding, 'Never heard a possum that could sing, and an old war song at that.'

The thoughts about possums singing or timbers creaking were just a blip on the horizon, heralding an episode which caused restless nights, strange dreams, discoveries, a positive identification and a final fleeing from the flat.

Garth was a heavy sleeper and an early riser, with his alarm clock set for 5.30 a.m. Time to wake, clear the head, rub his eyes, shower, shave and change, then drive off to his work site for the day. Back home, he read some of my books till 11.30 p.m. and dozed lightly, thinking he heard a noise from the bedroom. He brushed the thought aside and staggered to his bed confident the alarm clock would wake him. He sat up with a start when sunlight crept through the curtains. It was 8 a.m. and he panicked, driving quickly without having had any rest to his work site to be greeted by a grumpy boss. He received a curt warning and worked overtime without claiming it. He walked into the flat at 6.30 p.m., miffed about the clock, and checked it. The alarm button was pressed in on the old clock, which came with the flat.

'I was late for work. The clock didn't go off. The button is still in. Did you turn it off, Sharon?' His words had a hint of accusation.

'Bloody hell, Garth, of course not.'

It occurred to him that something was up. Someone or something wanted them out and gone. He put the alarm clock in a bucket and dragged a cement slab from the yard, placing it over the bucket. The TV blared to midnight. Sharon was in bed. He heard a thud and ran into the bedroom and there was the slab on the floor and Sharon still asleep. The windows were closed and it was a still night. Garth sat on the bed reading by torchlight and then the smell flooded in mingling in the atmosphere of cheroot smoke and roses. It was so strong that Garth coughed – he was not a smoker. He lifted his eyes from the book and saw her standing at the foot of the bed. She was tall. She was middle-aged and dressed in a World War II nurse's uniform with a red band on her hat. Her arms were folded and her blazing eyes stared straight into his face. He swallowed some saliva in a effort to yell to Sharon but nothing came out and he watched as the spirit slid alongside the snoring Sharon and pulled off her bedclothes. Sharon sat up looking angry at Garth, who was pointing to the right side. She turned her head and screamed, which caused the ghost to drift away. They sat up whispering to themselves and there she was again at the foot of the bed and pointing a waggling finger towards the wide-awake couple.

Garth plucked up his courage and picked up his shoe. He threw it at her and yelled, 'Piss off.'

Which she did.

Flats were hard to come by, and the couple were not prepared to be driven out. Sharon placed a beauty mask, with lemons, over her eyes and Garth pulled a balaclava over his head. Two more clocks were purchased and set at intervals. Nothing happened, so life went on.

John came to their flat and listened to their distress. He produced an old dog-eared album and opened it. There she was – the ghost of their flat and John's deceased wife. She looked younger then.

The teary-eyed man spoke. 'She died at fifty-four with cancer and I miss her even though she was a bit of a tyrant. The kids left. We sold the house and bought the two flats. This is where we lived and this is where she died. I am sorry. I thought she had gone on. The last couple fled out of here without paying the rent.'

'You should see a priest, John. She's trapped here.'

'I know. I've been avoiding it. I'm an atheist but I'm having doubts about that now.'

'We have to go, John. We can't stand the sleepless nights.'

'I'll find you a place today and help you move out. Stay in my house and I'll stay here for a while. OK?'

They agreed and within the week had found another house, some miles away from the Hillcrest Ghost

19

Publication

After my first book, *The Journey of Hamlin Baylis Wells*, was published, Grey Eagle was about the place a lot more and dreams came in. I wondered if, not being a celebrity, my autobiography would ever get up and on my walks I asked my dad for advice. It may have been him or Grey Eagle. My father died in 1974 and I was thinking about him a lot more on the walk.

I keep my eyes open and at times have found a lot of coins; I saw a 1974 five-cent piece on the footpath. I walked on a bit further and saw a ten-cent piece and the date was 1974. I almost tripped over a twenty-cent coin and it was 1974. I closed my eyes and two metres away was a fifty-cent coin, 1974. What is the likelihood of that sort of coincidence? I thanked whoever sent the signs to me. I knew the book would be published. And from then on the dialogue with Grey Eagle started in earnest and has continued. But the thought of even tiny bits of fame scared me from the moment I was told about it by Ray P.

Fame

I am not under the spell of fame and as a small banana in the world of writing I do not expect to have to cope with it. Fame does not come with an off/on button. There is in my perception a major problem with being famous, as in the world of a celebrity. How long before the real self is obscured by an unshakeable image which becomes a millstone? In time, fans circle, trying to touch their idol. The touch soon becomes a clutch, a tear of clothing with dopey fans calling out, 'I saw him first.' At that point the idol wishes he was somewhere else and wearing a mask. For the fans it is a hollow victory, just a small way to satisfy their own need and their own perception of themselves. It has reached a madness in our world created by the media, with hysterical people intent on basking in the glory, name dropping and meeting other famous people within the highest order of the circle. The idol is doomed to isolation when he becomes dependent on the people who infect him by feeding on him, like emotional vampires, which in turn inflates their own egos. He feels like he is falling over a waterfall and being dashed on giant rocks. The idol is drawn into a world of me-me-me, incapable of sustaining a normal relationship because of his boosted ego which needs to feel superior to lesser mortals.

And how the ego thrives with the role playing which can only lead to an addiction or years of therapy sometimes in a sanatorium and hooked on morphine-based tablets. He might never realise who he has become. In time, those people who felt the touch of fame (if only for a brief moment) would wish the clock could be turned back.

20

Conversations With Grey Eagle

'Hi, GE. Are you there?' I wrote.

I must have struck him on bad day – he tells me that some days are not up to scratch.

'Don't write silly questions. I am always here. What is the problem?'

'Not a problem. Just wanted to thank you for sending me the message about SM. Turns out to be Stephen Matthews the publisher.'

'Thanks for that but I knew, as you're aware. It was not locked in concrete, though, when he would move to Adelaide.'

'I will never doubt the spirits again. Just like you said, signs and dreams.'

'Glad you joined the group?'

'Would never have met Stephen if I hadn't. Publishers were not exactly knocking my door down, you know.'

'He is going to help your group and at least several more of your books will come out.'

'Bloody hell.'

'I was with you all the way with Hamlin, you know.'

'Of course. I still have the notes.'

'It's really you, Raymond, isn't it, without the obsessions and the confessionals?'

I didn't reply. I already knew he was there helping even when the draft had to be altered.

'It's all about a rumour in the police, isn't it?'

Yes, I thought, but he knows that, and he read my mind once again.

'We don't know everything up here, you know.'

I once again did not reply. But the scribble started again.

'I am glad you took my advice and set it in another state just in case someone thought you were writing about them and started civil action.'

I replied again in writing, 'Well, I changed the names as well just in case... I knew him, you know. I thought you might have guessed that. He was with us on the army games up north.'

'I did know. Do you know that I was standing alongside you at the library when you were doing your research about the setting in Brunswick? You picked up a book which I guided to you.'

'I felt a breeze and then the back of my head was itchy.' I waited for a reply which I knew might be humorous and it was.

'Might be dandruff. We can fix that for you.'

I chuckled but thought to ask him about his life on earth. 'Which tribe did you belong to?'

I saw the wiggly lines and the loops coming fast and spreading out.

'The Sioux, and to pre-empt your next question, I served under the great Red Cloud.'

'He of the famous sayings. I loved the one with the sting in the tail: the white man made many promises and broke them all except one – he promised to take our land and he did.'

'Very good, Raymond. Your memory is excellent at times. I am proud of you and will tell him when I see him. I was there when he said that.'

I was not prepared to ask him if he took scalps or any of the other stuff which we heard about and went onto another subject.

'So you like Somerset Maugham and his approach to *Razor's Edge*?'

I started to write my answer again. 'Yes. He writes about the parade of people who take on life whether or not those paths bring them satisfaction. He demonstrates how people really move through actions and dreams. He nails it with the varying view of the purpose of existence. I'm trying to guess what the purpose is and hope you'll oblige, GE.'

'Try to do good things everyday. There is no rush into a state of goodness every minute unless you feel the need on some days.'

I was mindful of his advice and thought back to Hamlin, who turned his back on the world of a police detective when he failed to hand in the huge amount of money found after a drug bust. His conscience prevailed and led him on another path of spirit. But that part was not me. I would have handed it in from the outset because it was contaminated money.

Maybe afterwards I might have thought, just pull out enough to pay the mortgage. But I also knew something else I would not have done and that was sort of sit on a mountain counting my toes, because life has too much to offer. There are people to meet and people to help if they need it.

Once, I put a few questions to a born-again man who thought I was dealing with Satan with my views. 'What happens to Buddhist babies who will never know Jesus?' The answer shocked me.

'They can't enter heaven.'

Which totally fixed any idea that I had about the Charismatic churches, even though I loved their gospel singing.

GE again: 'Brush up on your grammar.'

I took his advice and found a book in the library with that advice.

I searched back to the point where I had still shadows of doubt which followed me about, unmovable. But I learnt to make it disappear by shining a light on it. A light in the form of close meditation.

'You need a bit more grace, Raymond. The instant grace which you expect is fraught with problems. It can't come overnight like ordering a hamburger with all of the trimmings.'

'My god, Grey Eagle, how right is that?'

'Just look around for sources to inspire you. Don't ever forget that.'

'You're preaching to the converted.'

'No, just giving reinforcement.'

Reincarnation

I wanted his view on the subject which had perplexed Western nations for many years. I knew he must be a believer because of his life with Red Cloud. He wrote a narrative which appears to be credible and three-quarters of the world think the same.

Stella Derwood had a very long session one night at her house and we were asked to breathe deep and imagine that we were crowded together in a lift. We were to press the button. That I did, and ended in ancient Sparta.

I was in my home. I could smell the cooking of onions and home-baked bread. Roast chicken was about to be served, which turned out to be my last meal. Two women were there, one blonde and the other dark, who I recognised as women in my current life. I ate the meal and kissed them goodbye and marched away with others to the pass. We were to hold back the Persians. In the shower of arrows, I received a mortal wound.

I imagined I was back in the lift and pressed the button and came out into a world of cannon fire and saw the signpost SHILOH and looked at my grey uniform with the insignia on the sleeve, denoting I was a captain in the Confederate army. I turned just as a soldier on a horse rode me down and sliced my head open with a sabre. I felt the warm blood trickling down my face and also felt my pulse slowing and once again the blackness came over me. I was a bit sceptical with this as I was a student of the Civil War and had read many stories of the battles. I also saw *300 Spartans*, a film that remained in my mind, so I was not totally convinced. The jury is out about past lives.

However, Grey Eagle took another direction. 'Raymond, we will talk about this at a later point. I want to tell you now, we have reached a point where I can back off a bit. It is not student and teacher now. Participation, as you humans say. Call me if you need me. You have your psychic hotline.'

'OK. I'll let you return to your tepee.'

He didn't answer, probably thinking, 'Smart arse.'

21

Walk the Talk

'For as a man thinketh in his heart, so he is.' – Proverbs 23:7

Walking is wonderful. For the writer it is especially good because it clears away all the cobwebs, places us in the now, plucks out the feelings, the plots, the scenes and the paragraphs, with lots of similes. As anyone will tell you, I love similes, which add the sauce to the script. I say a prayer to God before I tie up the laces of my New Balance walkers (tied twice) and put on my sunnies and a hat, and the sun cream, and pick up the brolly if it looks like rain, and off I go, negotiating barking dogs, dog poo and joggers who think they own the pavement, and last of all I turn off the mobile, if I remember to take it. All I really lack is a rear-vision mirror, which I might invent one day. Perhaps I will get a glimpse of Grey Eagle if I do. Until I discovered him, I was not aware that I had a constant spirit companion (everyone does actually). I could have asked him a lot of questions before the publishing rejections came in but I had to learn lessons, so the rejections helped on my journey. However, I now know a lot more about dreams and signs, symbols, synchronicity and the hard world of publishing books. My chats have been heavily laced with automatic writing, as some of the preceding chapters showed.

After I went for a walk, I remembered a vivid dream. The setting was a lake, a peaceful location with only the sounds of water lapping the edges, a slight breeze and leaves rustling, only broken when I tossed pebbles into the lake. Grey Eagle wasn't there until I summoned him when the dream stopped, yet I was still asleep. In the middle of my peaceful pebble throwing, the scene changed to a beach location. It was a seaside hotel and I was in a beer garden without a canopy. Poker machines were lined up on the edge of an embankment and other people were playing them.

I slid a note into the machine and it burst into flames. I placed some coin in the slot and the bells rang immediately, signifying I had won a jackpot. Coins started pouring into the metal tray and overflowed, with fine bird seed mixed in amongst the coin. I struggled with pulling the seed away from the coin. The seed fell into a hole in the sand and started to sprout while I was retrieving the coin. The machine started to tip on its side and I moved away. A woman yelled out, 'Make sure the manager doesn't catch you – he'll blame you for breaking the machine.' I took off. I examined it, still in that dream, and came to a conclusion. It was about writing. Seeds pouring out told me I had planted them; the note burning was money burning a hole in my pocket. Maybe hold onto what you have. Alternatively it might just be a warning about gambling.

The dream faded and I was still asleep in the peaceful place and called out to Grey Eagle. I sensed him behind me.

'Sorry to drag you out of your tepee.' I could feel his anger rising – he has told me over the months that anger can happen to guides as well.

'That's the second time you've said that.'

'So where do you live?'

'In a crystal palace. Let me explain to you, the tepee is there in case any of my tribe come over. It allows them to adjust.'

'So I'm not the only one then?'

'At the moment you are. You see, you were part of my tribe.'

I thought about this; it reinforced his belief in past lives and to a degree got me thinking as well.

'When did I die?'

'In 1836.'

'How old was I?'

'About sixteen.'

'What was I like?'

'You were very lazy. In fact, so lazy that you went to sleep with a fly on your nose.'

'Very impressive, GE. How did I die?'

'You were killed by music.'

'Music! How did that happen?'

'By the drumming, the percussion if you like, of the hooves of buffalo. You were, as usual, asleep near the herd.'

I chuckled a bit at his humour and formed another question. 'Did I come back to earth soon after?'

'Look, it's not a revolving door, you know. But yes, you came back to the same country in 1840, born into a wealthy Southern family.'

My ears started to prick up then and I did a bit of calculating. 1840. Add twenty-one years, the Civil War, Southern boy, Confederate, probably cavalry. And I remembered the experiment with the lift in 1978 with Stella.

'Was I a Confederate cavalry man killed at Shiloh?'

'Doubting Thomas again. Of course. Stella was right. Trust anything which comes immediately into your head. Tell me why you think you grew up thousands of miles away from the USA with such an obsession about the Civil War? And didn't the teacher at your high school want you to be a history teacher?'

'Hell, I forgot all about that.'

'You've forgotten quite a bit, Raymond.'

I changed the subject, not wishing to dwell on some of my past mistakes. 'The dream I had about the poker machines and my assumptions…are they accurate?'

'They're a warning to be careful about playing those infernal machines. They've ruined many of our tribe in Las Vegas and driven them to drink again. Didn't I say to you that we are now a team just sharing opinions without much teaching from me?'

'Yes, you did. But thanks anyway for all of your help.'

I woke up and still recall the excellent dream without recourse to notes.

22

Some Evidence

'It is not a matter of will, or will not. Everything is a choice: choose wisely' – Ed Hillenbrand

Stop for a while. Take a breather. If you have read everything so far, you might still have some doubts if you are not familiar with this material. If you are happy to read on, then that is fine. However, some of you may have already decided to consign the book to a cardboard box which is clearly marked FOR THE LOCAL NURSING HOME in your steadfast belief that you are not going there for a while, or not passing over for a while. (Do you know how to make God break into fits of laughter? Tell him your plans.) Or you may just return the book to the library and switch on *Master Chef*. But maybe, just maybe for your own sense of closure, consider that I might just have got it right. You might leave the telly off and read the rest of what this book has to say, bearing in mind my work with the judiciary, over a fifteen-year period, which gives some credibility to my words.

I worked on many country circuits with the courts. One of those involved nearly a week away from home. Faith M was the court reporter to Magistrate Michael F. I got on well with both of them. Faith was New Age and knew a lot about the afterlife. The nights away were spent with a quick meal at a pub and lazing around under the veranda of a local motel talking, drinking, telling jokes and much laughter. During those chats, which led to Faith's and my favourite subject, our magistrate spoke about a judge of the High Court in NSW who had written a book about the topic.

Victor Zammitt carried out a lifelong investigation of psychic phenomena, after having moved from an ingrained sharp sceptic to a total believer in the afterlife. His book has a lengthy title and is still available on a website, I am assured: *A Lawyer Presents a Case for the Afterlife – The Irrefutable Objective Evidence*. He retired from the bench and became a well known lecturer on that phenomenon. Much science is included within the pages and at the end, his sponsors, on their website, offer the sum of US one million dollars for anyone, anywhere, who can demonstrate that the evidence for the afterlife, as published on the Internet, is not correct. The magistrate told us the money remains unclaimed. Now that is putting your money where your mouth is. No scientist has yet produced evidence that the afterlife does not exist. But I guess some would answer as usual, 'But we are working on it.' My friend and former colleague would be smiling at these words from where she is now, having died tragically some time back, far too young.

I still have a book that has some of the binding breaking away, which tells me that it has passed through many hands, and it occurs to me it came from Faith. She left the job and moved to Queensland and then died, so I guess I am still the owner of it.

Followers of Eckankar use a mantra at the start of their meditations. It is their take on the way to God. They simply chant hu (pronounced like the man's name, Hugh) and focus on the third eye between the eyebrows. Within a short space of time, they lose all awareness of physical surroundings but their inner voice tells them when their thirty minutes of the mantra is up. It is all about practice, about providing time for the body to slow and beat in time with the soul. I have tried it (for a shorter period) and it works, not unlike yoga. Spiritual exercises are a matter of discipline. It is the love of the act and not the effort we make to improve ourselves which counts and the effort ought to be effortless.

23

Q and A

'Faith is the substance of things hoped for, the evidence of things not seen' – Hebrews 2:1

The puzzle of how I was fast tracked into the publishing world stayed in my brain because the essentials required by publishing firms, whose rules are so strict that a first-time writer, without an agent (the number of agents in South Australia ready to take on new work is almost zero and those who are here are fairly precious anyway), or without some reviewer's assessment attached (at a $2,000-dollar fee, do you mind), is designed to throw any new prospective writer with his eye on the Great Australian Novel off the scent before he gets to first base. It is the reason why many new writers turn to online stuff in an endeavour to market their book, which is a path to bitterness when you find out that much of it is self-publishing, with outrageous promises made and never kept. Most give up. However, I didn't.

Those with money who are prepared to self-publish sometimes take that road: many of them are stuck with hundreds of books which they can't sell. It's all about marketing at the end of the day. Marketing before the launch, putting out invitations to friends and relatives who make promises they can't keep. Organising the night, which is akin to a wedding reception, having a good venue (think about the price and the catering). Asking someone in the trade if they will introduce you and that means that they have to spend their time in preparation. And surprise, surprise, surprise, like Gomer Pyle used to say, you have to give a speech and make sure you get it right. And most of your audience is free to criticise without a clue of what you have gone through. Half the people you send out invites to will not turn up if a favourite TV show is on. Or if it's raining.

The blogs are put out and the pre advertising is OK but, unless they have heard of you, those who turn up will eat your grub, laugh at your jokes and leave without buying a book and ask later if they can read it at the library, to which you have donated a book at your expense. It's not over yet. The small print-on-demand publisher will expect you to buy some books at a discount and plough around banging on the doors of all those friends and rellies who said they would come.

You are like the Avon lady now, trying to sell your wares, just to keep your name on the publisher's website. If you're still interested, then you are made of the right stuff and you might just get on with another book, which is how I did it. It's about finally being savvy. However, I had a lot of help from my guide and there is no reason why you, the reader and possible writer, can't jump onto my coat tails. Serendipity worked for my writers group (NEW Inc) as well when Stephen Matthews came on the scene, searching for new, raw, material, and by God didn't he get some. I'm not moaning; I am a small banana in the writers' world and money has never been the way forward for me.

However, I am also pragmatic, because if a movie producer offered me a contract for one of my manuscripts, I would be there with my ears back, sniffing the air like an old fox, looking for a good dinner and checking out the surroundings. Like, has he got a bigger cave than me, and can I have one of those as well? So it goes, but I'm still here, having waited for a crash or to be slaughtered at a launch, still with itchy fingers which I can't stop, like a kitten dancing on the keys.

I ploughed on, dismissive of what other unpublished writers' problems were. Those poor sods waiting to be recognised with time passing them by, while people with red blood in their veins just forge on, putting out endless manuscripts, to dull the pain of rejections and lift themselves out from under the limbo stick, forcing the grammar to resonate.

The urgency of my question sent back a message from the world of dead writers: 'You have the ability to clothe your messages in a language easily understood by the common man.' And people with only a few minutes to spare, able to read a two-hour book.

The message is, we live on after death and my faith is irretrievable regarding that issue. Humans love to attach labels to others, almost like they can't live without slotting someone else in a folder. My handle is a mix of gnosticism, juiced up with Christianity, mixed in a brew of good old Buddhism which has unleashed some old demons: I am free of labels from now on. I should have recognised the help I was getting from beyond the veil because some of the words came into clear dreams. Words I might never have used. The reality behind that bugged me. Like, why me? And why at this age? Why not in earlier years? The answer came down the wire with a flurry of automatic writing, mediums, signs, dreams which flooded my cells every night, with the same old stuff. To top it off, what was written after my begging question was clear and concise: 'Timing, Raymond. You were not ready with all of the dramas in your life.' Isn't that the truth?

I knew what to write when the plot was sealed in my first book *The Journey of Hamlin Baylis Wells*. I had the bones there: I had met many Buddhists before, and was aware of the views which gave a voice to Hamlin when he went on a retreat with the peaceful people. But there were some gaps and they were filled with dreams of certain phrases.

'Mum, Dad and the Kombi'

A short story of 4,000 words, this was sent to a competition on Phillip Island and didn't go anywhere. I brushed it up and re-sent it to the SA Writers Festival in conjunction with the state government and Wirra Wirra Wines, supported by the Onkaparinga Council. This is a prestigious affair and one of the judges was Michael Bollen, the owner of Wakefield Press in Adelaide. No one was more surprised than I when the SA Writers Centre rang in August 2011 telling me I was one of the ten best picked to have their entries published in an anthology. I was buoyed by the news and appeared with the others in the anthology *Where's Pluto*.

24

Andrew Cox and the Ghost of Fitzroy

'For all of our insight, obstinate habits do not disappear
until replaced by other habits.'

Andrew Cox is a solidly built man in his early forties with two sons. One lives in the place of his birth in New Zealand. Andrew has resided in Australia for some time and is the husband of my daughter Kerry. He is a gas turbine artificer and currently works as a contract youth worker, which is not without its nightly dramas due to the nature of social work and all the issues which follow on from that calling. I chuckle at his hobby of collecting all sorts of material which he generally restores and sells, either on ebay or at garage sales. Many of my friends are engaged in that hobby, which at times is quite profitable. Andrew is also Mr Fix-it and a handyman, which reminds me of my father, who could also fix anything. Anyone reading this short bio would assume correctly that he is not easily scared. However, the events which occurred during 1995 in Brunswick Street, which sits in the suburb of Fitzroy, shook his usually steady foundations.

He shared an upstairs flat in a winding street in that suburb of Melbourne. Both the young people had jobs that kept them busy. Andrew had three jobs and not much time on his hands, as he frequently worked into the early hours of the morning. Dead tired, happy to slump on the bed, chucking his keys in the same place on a kitchen table, waiting for a quick morning getaway. It was complicated, with neither of them having time to just sit, think, read or watch the TV in the old 1890s house which might have promised a ghost or two.

The troubles started one morning. The keys were dumped in the same place but next morning around 7 a.m. they were gone. In a frantic search to find them, they found the keys on the lounge but thought no more about it.

Unfortunately it kept on happening, along with clothes such as hats, shirts pullovers, which also disappeared from their allotted space and were not located, even with a thorough search. Andrew believed quite strongly that someone might have entered through the roof space but the search proved nothing. It was now down to something supernatural, but no time was available for the couple to commence some research. They had enough and decided to move. Both agreed that a spirit hovered, not happy about the new invaders. Furniture was shuffled around just before the move. It was then that Andrew found the missing clothes, stuffed behind an old heavy dressing table.

A few nights before their move, Andrew woke from a heavy sleep feeling someone or something was watching him. He rubbed his eyes and stared at the end of the bed just as a shadow and then a figure appeared staring down at him. His mouth was dry, which caused him to swallow at the sight of the bulky figure dressed in black with her hair tied up in a bun. She was a matronly-looking person dressed just like woman from the Victorian era. Her hands were clasped behind her back. She did not speak, she just glared with angry eyes cast down towards him, moving in closer, ever closer.

He felt very cold in spite of the blankets and smelt the faint smell of lavender. He closed his eyes, which were still blocked with the sleep gathered in the corners, invading his eyelashes, and then the courage came back. He opened them. The apparition had vanished.

During the days in their new place, he often wondered how long she was earthbound and how she died. Perhaps she was murdered and no one investigated it. The thoughts rambled about, buzzing like a wasp trapped in a spider's net. But who could he report it too? And more importantly, would they believe him? And in the hurly burly rush of the world, the thoughts passed away.

The sighting is the only one Andrew ever saw with such clarity. However, his intuition is high because he lives in an old house and at times hears a few inappropriate groans. He turns over and goes back to sleep with the thought, why bother? Maybe it's the wind. Or maybe it's not. Or is it Kali?

25

Don't Mess With Kali

'Men are disturbed not by a thing which happens, but by the opinion about the thing.' – Enchiridion (ancient seer)

Andrew Cox never forgot the power of Kali, the Hindu goddess of death and destruction, whose followers called the Thuggees murdered thousands of innocent travellers in India since AD1290. His New Age shop in Melbourne in the 1990s was his pride and joy and spurred daily research which was needed to accurately inform his customers, those who needed to know the legends of the stones and the gems, the tarot and the carved statues of deities which lined his shelves. Kali the Goddess took pride of place with a price tag of $35. He was aware of her power, and her eyes followed him, almost swivelling when he walked past, which occasionally gave him goosebumps. If it was necessary to touch her, he made sure to wash his hands before and after. The carving was not an object to be messed with.

Sitting near her on the shelf were newspapers from Madras in 1889. The reader would be fascinated and a bit squeamish with the photos of seven bodies of Thuggees dangling from a gallows and a British major watching. Major William Sleeman was the hunter of the now-dead men and proclaimed in an ego-driven report how he had brought them to justice. The article was full of the words from an Anglo-Saxon brain which required closure, victory and a triumph for the Empire – how they met their painful end in a twenty-minute twitching strangulation, and justice had been done. The cult was no more – so he thought. The Indian people drew a different conclusion: that the worship of Kali still thrived 800 more or less years later.

Andrew Cox was busy in his New Age shop. He was distracted for a few seconds when a young woman near the statue of Kali hurried out of the shop. He found just an empty space where Kali had stood and became angry but resigned. At the end of the day, it drifted into his thoughts how the thief might have a lot more trouble after the theft – trouble she could not even guess about – with Kali and her swivelling eyes illegally in her home. He was friendly with a frequent customer who was a senior sergeant of police and a buyer of many goods. They were chatting in a corner about three weeks after the theft when a man walked quickly into the shop, with a bulge under his shirt. A quick glance revealed the man removing the statue of Kali. He placed it on the shelf, glanced back towards Andrew and saw the officer in the blue uniform. The man charged out of the shop.

'What's that all about, Andrew?'

Andrew explained the whole story about the woman and the theft.

'Do you want me to follow it up, mate?'

'No. his conscience tells the story. Crikey, they must have had a few bad moments.'

He thanked Kali. Not that he was a devotee or believed it. He just wanted to keep his options open.

26

NDE and OBE

'You must not lose faith in humanity. Humanity is an ocean. If a few drops of ocean are dirty, the ocean does not become dirty.'

– Mahatma Gandhi

Have I touched a nerve somewhere which made you jump and, hopefully, started a germ of an idea within you, about the phenomena of NDE and OBE? Or is it old hat, because of the staggering amount of books, movies and accounts, which appear to run the same account without any change. An account of running or crawling down a tunnel with a great big light at the end and some celestial being says 'Go back.' Stand-up comedians are still getting their fourpence-worth out of the jokes. And I opine that the great source has a giggle or two about the adaptability of his creations

The Big One

There wasn't a fancy handle for an NDE or an OBE in 1958, because those blessed few who died or were at the point of death (and found out it is not blackness, which always makes me smile because black is a colour which is seen by the naked eye, so it is something) usually kept their epiphany to themselves because of the fear of ridicule or an involuntary holiday within the closed environment of a mental hospital. Frontal lobotomy was popular with the men in white, who used scalpels, buzz saws and lots of therapy during that time; and lots of sleeping pills, providing the nursing staff with more comfortable time in the wards so they could write their daily notes on the board at the end of the bed, which always said, 'The patient slept well.' Of course he did, because with only half a brain and buckets of pills he was away most nights on an OBE. So I shut up as well. There were no idle chats with others about my NDEs (and their poorer cousins OBEs).

The big one started after an accident, an electrocution, caused by shabby workshop practices, involving the use of extension leads without an earth pin. I was in great pain, supine, under a semi-trailer with the big electric drill churning away, shaking my whole body with surges. I must have looked like a dog which had swallowed a packet of razor blades. Two hundred and forty volts yanked my elbows, knees and neck out of joint and I could not yell for help, such were the paralysing effects of the electricity. My heart raced, pounding in my chest to a point where I thought it would burst away from its twenty-four-year-old moorings.

I passed out at that point just as my heart slowed from a lub dub lub dub to a lub, slowing like a horse whose gallop has gone from a canter to a trot and a stop. I didn't look down. I was drowning. A racing freedom took hold. I dashed along a green tunnel head-first towards a bright blinding light, much like gazing into the sun. I knew I was dead then, because I couldn't see, dangling behind, the silver cord which always came with me on my conscious journeys in the many past OBEs. An emotion came into my being (and not from the brain, as I had been down the tunnel for over six minutes): I was happy, released from cares. No longer having to go to the same pub for something to do and listen to a bunch of drunken yobbos shrieking with laughter about which female they had screwed during the week. The racing movement stopped and I stood and walked on. I did not see anyone I knew on the walk, though many couples were moving about with animals and children. I saw no period costumes, so this was not another time.

A voice came to me. It wrapped itself all around my dirty overalls and clearly said, 'You are going back, Raymond. There is much to do. Remember this all of your life and now know you are protected.'

Hands turned me around and I walked back, this time to where my body lay, and the ambulance men were loading my form on a stretcher. People stood around with solemn faces until I sat up, jumped down and told the boss I was going home. A taxi took me home and I never went back to that job. I did not speak about it either or make any claims. Did I lead a life of celibacy, swear off drink and stop telling yarns? Sorry to disappoint you: no, an emphatic no. However, my conscience was much clearer. I was not inclined to treat others as insignificant and, above all, I knew that we pass to another world, a belief which has remained unshakeable in my memory. How easy it is to lose a life in a flash and how precious life is.

The episode caused within me an obsession to read much literature that is referred as New Age. I found enough evidence to quell the doubting part of the brain. There is a plethora of evidence about an afterlife. We are sent here to learn lessons. An article called 'The Dutch Study' by Pym Van Lommel, an eminent cardiologist, was published in the British *Lancet* medical journal. He came down on the side of yes, NDEs and OBEs are true. Not fake. That is only one of many others by scientists. So it goes, and as far as I know my brain is still intact in spite of being out of operation after four minutes. However, the point missed by the atheists is that it is not the brain which is working after the shut down. It is that mysterious part called the soul, which doesn't need a battery and an engine to keep it going. It knows all and is co-joined with the ether of the world.

OBE

I am wiser now, thanks to Grey Eagle, who has presented with me the germ of how it all works and glimpses, tiny at times, of past lives. However, I won't state that all glimpses, with lucid dreams, are about an OBE. There is, though, a study which declared ten per cent to twenty per cent of the population (in the USA) have OBEs and NDEs. The connecting point of difference between NDE and OBE is that OBE people are still conscious and the spontaneous escape from the body is usually involuntary, though some yogis are practised in the art of being to negotiate it with their will.

Dream studies have concluded that when we wake with a sudden jolt after a vivid lucid dream we have had an OBE and the thud is the return back into the physical body.

I believe the NDE and the OBE can overlap. I didn't seem to float out; just everything became a continuous event, flowing on sequentially. Maybe it would be better to call my experience a death experience. Some OBEs could turn into a NDE or a death experience. In my OBE stuff as a child I was at times in a delirious state and also fully awake when I saw my body lying there coughing while I was coming down from the ceiling watching my parents wringing their hands.

I have no doubt that LSD and similar drugs would induce an OBE, even a traumatic incident. For instance, the following narrative occurred some years back when I was recovering from a bad dose of tonsillitis and had an X-ray. After the X-ray I was required to return an hour later and I had time to kill.

The Museum

I was in the Egyptian room in the SA Museum in Adelaide and it was near closing. The musty smell seemed to grow heavier when the lights went dim. I gazed down at the coffin of a highly decorated young prince: I was busy reading the script about his life and smelling the mud, the murky water and a strong scent of spices. A fleeting shadow sat in a corner and it was then that I felt spooked. I gasped and tried to blow away the smell but it twirled like a dust storm engulfing me, coming close, ever closer into my vision.

I was transported back in time and saw myself walking along a stone path. My hands were tied behind my back and I was quite young. There were lash marks on my back. I had the feeling that I was walking to my execution. I saw a block in the distance and a huge man holding a heavy blade. I was to be decapitated. I was shoved down on the block face first and then yelled out, 'Help.' Blood and blackness followed. I woke up sprawled on top of the coffin with the twentieth-century century guard shaking me.

'Are you OK?' Concerned, he walked with me to the door. 'You're not the first person who has had this experience in that room.' He looked a bit spooked himself.

Later in life I concluded that it was probably a past-life moment happening.

1789 (a lucid dream)

I clearly heard the rumble of the tumbrel which I was in with a couple of other people. I was holding the hand of a delicate mid-teens girl who was dressed in fine linen which was stained with urine, steadily trickling down to the tattered hem of her dress. We saw the great blade ahead and watched while another victim's body was cast aside like a stray dog. My friend shivered but held her body straight, which gave to me a sudden rush of bravery when I mounted the steps.

I felt the straps pulled tight over the rat bites and knew I would soon be in a better place. The blade was raised and it squeaked and I remember thinking, it needs oiling, hope it falls quickly.

I prayed while the blade was being unsnagged and I got as far as 'Hallowed be thy name.' In that moment, my body whooshed out, or something did, and I saw my head fall into the basket while I stood at the top of the platform with a full body, realising I was alive but in another plane. She was next and there we were walking off together holding hands and meeting with her parents. I looked back once and saw the cart being loaded with bodies. Mine and the girl's.

The dream or whatever it was filled me with terror, yet a lot of love and freedom from pain and decadence. However, I can't say I have ever met her in this life, though I wish I had, and while I am on that subject, Grey Eagle laughs at the oft-used expression 'soulmates'.

Oh and yes, I woke up with such a start and a loud crack, which told me when I was shaving that it was an OBE and probably a true account of my death in 1789.

However, there is no point listing every dream I have had, because every human has them, though they fail to interpret them upon waking.

27

Upsetting the Apple Cart

*'As cold water to a thirsty soul; so is good news from a far country' –
Proverbs 25:25*

Writing a non-fiction book with controversial themes – automatic writing to a spirit guide and getting answers; dreams, signs, synchronicity, hauntings; getting advice from mediums at spiritualist churches; finding evidence of an afterlife; and last of all reincarnation – is bound to upset the apple cart of conventional churches and non-believers but do I care? You bet your sweet bippy, I don't. Those interested enough to read all of this book might treat it like a Christmas cake, possibly too rich and too dense for some readers. Yet others may be inspired to search their own chapters for the life force which lies behind the science of the mind and the personality. The accumulation of vast amounts of literature which I have read over the last forty years, all speaking about the possibilities of intentions, dreams and manifestations, really came down to little. I was stuck like a steam train in a station with a head full of steam bursting at the seams waiting for the engineer to push the lever into forward motion and then race away fulfilling the mission.

Hindsight tells me that in spite of all my endeavours I had reached a stage where the signposts were all turned around by some unseen hand saying, 'Going the wrong way, Raymond. Write to us, tell us and we will write back.' It seemed to me at that point I was like a fisherman closeted inside a fur-lined waterproof to keep away the cold and the salty winds with a full moon watching, tossing out static electricity which spooked him. I was spooked but it stopped when I started to write down my questions and wait for answers and, brother, didn't they arrive, as you have found out over the last pages.

I posed a question once to GE about reincarnation: 'What is achieved by doing past-life regressions?'

This was the answer which came out clearly in his bold writing: 'The hypnotic regression has many good sides to it. It can assist with the gaining of great knowledge and talents which were built in past lives. It can mend the phobias so that the knot can be permanently straightened out. Artistic and even medical skills may surface, but the main positive is the purging of old built-up garbage.'

'Does the cycle of life after life ever end?'

'Yes, it does but let me say you have discovered a piece of yourself ever since we first started out, Raymond. Work on those pieces to join up the jigsaw which is part of your quest. It is a thing you lost once and you will find it again. Once found, it will straighten out the kinks and you may then look to another life well beyond your present little corner of security. Do not lecture people around you about your new-found knowledge unless they want to engage with you about it. Drop those people who openly criticise your path. Once you begin the new journey, the snails will hold you back but they will be outpaced by your rapid strides. Their dream is not your dream. Your focus from now is to be with God, survive and then go home.'

The session was closed until spring 2012. I had other short books to write as well as launches to attend with other writers in my group. I sat poised with a new pen and fresh paper. I needed to ask GE about his life rather than mine and, as he helped, along with others, to get my works published, I felt I had best give up on anything more to do with publishing. After all, I had done well.

'Have you always been my guide, Grey Eagle?'

The pen paused for a short time. 'Yes, since 1936.'

I felt many questions coming on. 'Will you be my guide once I pass over?'

'No, I can elect to guide another but the option is to move to a higher realm, which I will take.'

I guessed maybe he was sick of me. 'Had enough of these last seventy-five years?'

'Your words, Raymond, not mine.'

Now it was onto him once more and his life. 'When did you die?'

'At the turn of the nineteenth century.'

'How did you die?'

'I had enough of Whiteman's reservations and I was old and wanted to be away from their flour and tea. I packed my buffalo-hide bag which my beloved dead wife hand-stitched for me many years ago and I walked away towards the snow-capped mountains.'

Thought about suicide entered into my writings so I was careful what I wrote next. 'So, did you find a place in the snow, in your tepee?'

'Yes, and it was there when I remembered how to induce a trance state. It worked well as an OBE, as you call them.'

'Did you speak to your guide at the time?'

'Yes, he was my great grandfather.'

I plucked up courage and held the pen tightly when I wrote, almost expecting a spirit tap across the back of my head. 'Did you will yourself to die?'

His answer was quick and written with the pen pushed down hard. 'No, I didn't will myself. I just followed the steps which enabled my body to shut down.'

'So what happened then?'

'I sat in the snow and shivered until warmth came over me. I looked into the stars and at the same time I felt my heart slowing. I looked back when my spirit body started to rise and saw the silver cord breaking. In a flash I was with my grandfather marching along towards the giant crystal castle.'

'And now for the big one, GE, which all humans want to know. Did you meet God on your journey?'

'The great spirit is always about. I have met him many times,' He added a few last words. 'Do not wait for the last judgement. It takes place every day.'

Since that time in December 2011, I have not queried him about books which might be published and I suspect on that matter I am left to my own devices.

Even if the past weighs us down and the old film of our life is clouded, in truth all we have is today, and all things are possible. In the busyness of life it is all too easy to realise what a precious gift each day is. It's important not to live *for* today, but to live *in* today.

Write the things which you have seen and the things which are, and the things which shall be. I know Grey Eagle is with me and I know more signs will come (about many matters which help in our human life). The question is, will a publisher take it all on board? I guess he would have to be a very open-minded person. Will I keep on writing as long as the body holds out and the bookends are not yet made? I am comfortable that more will come. Each new dawn starts a blank slate. The slate is not washed off because I took the advice of GE and wrote other tales from cop life, which included dramas encountered by my colleagues.

Part III

28

GE Is Back

2012 just evaporated and GE is back. I sense and smell his leathery odour in the bathroom and the dreams we share in this last round of writing are visual. Not that he spells it out chronologically, in perfect order. Mostly the scenes don't make sense at the time. They are like a Russian doll with replicas dotted inside. It is all metaphors and usually I get them right, once I dissect them. The anecdotes are a few left over and remembered after I had written the earlier parts of this book.

As far back as I can remember, I have had a vivid imagination. It caused a bursting ego in the late 1950 era when our police instructor, Senior Constable Wally Budd, a most eloquent man, pronounced to my classmates at the Thebarton training college that my essay, dredged from nothing, was the best he had read. It did not take long to discover that a little kudos delivered early in the piece was not a guarantee of a smooth ride through a police career. I needed more than a way with words and a smart mouth to succeed as an SA cop, which was apparent when we hit the streets and the books were virtually thrown away.

Appearances had to be kept up: no one must be seen without a hat or a tie, and the same rule applied to the general public. Everyone I knew had a job. No one spoke about the drop-outs who were either in gaol or in Parkside, which was the state's main mental institution. It was all melodrama, the good versus the bad, which was well promoted by the population's love of the movies. The main loves were *Gone with the Wind*, *Mrs Miniver*, John Wayne and *Rebecca*. We all kept our secrets close inside, including the police. No mention was made of the dreaded Big C, which was then called simply 'growths'. Yet people died in droves, which I soon found out as a serving cop. Sometimes five a week, who we carted to the morgue. Hanging was popular, as was the lash. Nil tolerance was given to street behaviour offences. Homosexuality was a capital offence and stayed underground until a future government removed the offence from the books.

I remember the line used by Wally Budd just before we were released onto the unsuspecting public. 'Believe me, gentlemen, you will unearth grubbiness, which has always lived in the shadows of the city, yet you will be expected, when called upon, to reveal yourselves in the protection of the citizens who you have sworn to protect. So I say do not harass those folk unless strictly necessary. Maybe be like blue ghosts who emerge, strike and fade back into the shadows.'

I was prepared for the grubbiness because I had encountered it in my life. I was unsure about the blue ghosts bit, though it was a good line.

That was 1957. I left the force later in 1958 for RAN Reserve commitments but failed the trade test. I was determined that if I did not make it back in the SA Police, I would join the Victoria force. I applied in 1958 for re-entry and was accepted in 1959. I was back in what I liked best.

I never went back to my trade and I think Dad was disappointed. Maybe he thought it was a waste of five years but nowadays I am older and a bit wiser and realise that nothing really is a waste. I believe we are where we should be at all times in life. I doubt that I would be writing and be published if the chips had fallen in a different fashion. If I have anyone to point the finger at when I have a rare look back at the what-ifs, I sometimes lay a bit of blame at GE's feet. I hope he is not reading this. If he is, I guess he will reflect, 'Well, that's Raymond the good talker, but not so much the good listener. Always too busy.'

29

Thinking Back

I was thirteen years of age when I rode my old Malvern Star pushbike on a silent journey with nothing but the crosswinds and the mooing cows grazing in the paddocks to distract my attention from the mission. The road was then the Mount Barker Road, which was the route through the Adelaide Hills and on to the bordering green state of Victoria. I was nearing the end of my journey near the quiet town of Crafers, which nestled amongst the tall deciduous trees providing comforting shade and cover for the folk who lived in the area.

My Auntie Mary Wakefield shared a house with Sid the Jewish man. The family cackled behind cupped hands about her visions. I didn't cackle and in spite of what GE said I listened to her relate her visions. Actually, once I found out about such phenomena, I knew she was a medium of some skill. However, society had a closed mind about the Marys of the world. Indeed, it was still on the books as a criminal offence and a well known medium spent some time in gaol for her readings. A detective who had stars in his crown and went out of his way to persecute her followed her about. Such was the black side of Adelaide society in those times. So much for the good old days.

The sound of the squeaky chain grinding away and frequently jumping off the sprocket could be heard above the wind. I jammed the chain back into place with a practised careful movement of my feet. It maintained my upward climb and I reassured myself by chanting out loud to the inanimate object, which obeyed my wishes like a faithful pet.

My thoughts jumbled about on the return journey to Glenunga, where my parents were staying, and how I could freewheel down (the brakes were in bad shape and I might have to help by holding my right foot against the tyre). My fingers had changed colour because of the cold air, and the chilblains which I suffered from had attacked my protruding ears. They flapped against my head with the change of wind direction. My ears looked like the flags waved by goal umpires in a football match, as a kid at school said. Another one called me Dumbo, so you can imagine I developed an obsession about my ears. Barbers were not allowed to pull them out of place because I found a way to reduce the size by sticking a rubber band around them in amongst the mop of lanky, almost white hair. (I was once named Snowy.) I forgot about the restrictive rubber band once at school. After it snapped quite loud, from then on I was told I was disruptive. In time my head grew bigger to match the ears and the obsession finally went away.

I rubbed my hands on the rubber handgrips and some warmth returned to my iced-up fingers. I was not about to be deterred from my task. Mum used to tell all that I was a very determined kid. I guess I would be called a lateral thinker. If I spot an obstacle ahead, I find a way around it. It can also be a curse as well as a blessing because I have made many financial mistakes in my life due to taking the wrong path. But that's life: just ask your guide. If he is like GE, you will know what I mean.

The bike trip was special because it was to honour the memory of my friend Peter Rewhip, who had met his death near Crafers when an out-of-control truck ran over him. On that fateful day, Peter had pushed on past Les Duncombe (who had married one of my cousins, which we didn't know then and was part of discoveries in 1980), past Mervyn and me, and we three turned back. We used to wonder, if we had ridden on, whether the truck would have killed us all. Such is the fragility of life on this planet and thanks to GE I have learned each day to bless what I have – it is simply called 'breath'.

Tears welled down my cheeks with the flashback of the good times and the bad. Peter was gone from our lives, along with the toys he made, his infectious smile and the silly limericks which we sang out of tune. I gathered my breath and sang our favourite in remembrance of our friend. A bawdy song. 'Everybody's doing it, doing it, doing it, picking their nose, chewing it, chewing it.' At the end of the ditty, I remembered how we coughed and laughed and how we were nearly sick when Dirty Mervyn picked a boogie in front of us all and ate it. I remembered the mentally challenged boy who walked to the same school as me, and who constantly had his fingers up his nose sampling the contents.

The OBEs which I had when I was seven and very close to death were subsiding. The tumbling swirling feeling which was a precursor to the event always scared me so much that I tried not to sleep but the moment I closed my eyes it started again. My last OBE happened the night before the journey in Peter's memory; he came to me, smiling as usual with that goofy smile and his big teeth. It reminded me of how the old man came out of the bushes, smiling and exposing himself and then ran away. We laughed about the old man with his dirty shirt and his dirty trousers all stained down the front. And Mervyn. the oldest of all, who, in an escape from a brutal father, constantly went into the shed and masturbated over the girlie magazines and told us how good it felt. He remarked when the old man ran away, 'He's been pulling himself.' We three looked at each other and had a collective thought, yes, Mervyn, and you are always doing it.

Peter faded away in my OBE like bits of fragmented sparks from a flickering fluorescent tube on its last legs. I flew back into my body and started to hum our tune once again. Right through my working life and personal life, it seemed to me that everybody I knew was fixated on doing something every second, minute and hour. 'No rest for the wicked,' Mum would always say, and she was the least wicked person I ever knew. The doings of people were largely a form of exercise which embraced them in the now: the concentration on the task was their unknown, unrealised byword.

People were like that, I mused later in life after much recall. I came to that conclusion after studying elements of the Buddhist faith and I later wrote about it in my first book. I remember a phrase in the books I read which was prominent: 'Think shoelace. Enjoy the tying of a bow. Enjoy the simple moment.' I kept many sayings in handwritten books which were sprinkled among some of my homespun stuff.

30

William Lawrence

I unearthed the discovery of my birth during my middle age and how those secrets were revealed has become a focus for the continuation of my journey. Part of the yarn concerns my maternal birth grandfather William Lawrence, who was a South Australian police officer in the 1920s. I milked stories from the Lawrence family historian Joy Dalgleish, who lives in Busselton in Western Australia and is my cousin. She was able to fill in some gaps about the legend which haunted William the cop. Auntie Doris Manser was the lady who changed my nappies before I went to the Clift family. She supplied the milk bottles to strengthen my baby frame. She kept me in raptures while she related family stories. I still see her even though she is in her nineties.

The story which has cycled around through the years is now part of the William Lawrence saga and tells how badly William suffered a bout of post-traumatic stress which caused his early departure from the police.

In the infancy of his career, when he was naive as most young cops are, he was assigned to a beat in Adelaide's west end, a place where razor gangs lived. Hindley Street was the pick-up point for the constable, who would be conveyed to the Adelaide gaol, where he was to be a witness, along with another cop, to the 8 a.m. execution of a man convicted of murder. There were no beg-your-pardons or worming out.

'Stand under the gallows, you two, and wait for my signal,' ordered the sheriff, who wore military medals from many wars.

The drop of eight feet was measured before the manacled man was marched out with his arms pinioned and made to stand on the chalked spot on the trapdoor. A white hood was placed on top of the shivering man's head .The knot was fixed along the left side of his jawbone, under his ear, with a ring slip securing the knot.

'Ready, boys. Steady, wait,' said the sheriff and the men knew they were not just witnesses.

The condemned man was asked if he had any last words. William could not recall if he heard them but he heard the white hood snap down over the man's pale face. The huge trapdoor squeaked and opened with a great thud which was the point at which William always woke, screaming, after a dream. The man fell straight down but his legs wobbled and then lifted up. They heard him gurgling.

'Now, now with me. Grab his legs.'

And they did and the three held him till he became still. But not before the gasping sounds faded out. Severance of the spinal chord, which is supposed to result in instant death, had not worked. The sentence 'hanged by the neck until dead' always protected the executioner, because bodies remained for thirty minutes to ensure that the law of the land had been carried out. William insisted through his life that he had helped to kill a man he did not know and was finally released from the department without any pension or 'sorries'.

I have read the official account of the execution which was obtained by Joy D and there are no reports which might suggest there was a hiccup. The authorities in many areas kept secrets and the saga will probably remain a legend. Today, they would not have gotten away with it. An independent team of CSI people would have proved that the execution was badly managed. I have been against hanging as a death sentence since then. I am open on the subject of serial killers and the method of fatal injection, though I am yet to be convinced.

William and I never met. He died in 1958, well before I knew of him. However, I found out he was a head Masonic man and his daughter Doris told me that he knew I was a cop, which was confirmed in a conversation – puzzling at the time – in 1958. I was at St Peters police station when I spoke to Sergeant George Russell, who was a Mason.

'Nice to meet you, Ray. William Lawrence sends his regards.'

I just nodded without knowing what he meant, but many years later I understood exactly. GE told me so in a patch of writing on 9/11. We were on a holiday in Cairns when the screen burst out the drama. I was silent on the journey back in the ski lift and felt compelled to tackle some auto writing and there it was. The story never really ends.

31

Blue Ghosts

A situation occurred on my first night shift when I was stationed at No. 9 (City) Division. It was a time when we were left to our own devices and it came to pass when I changed from day shift to a night beat. The previous week was spent entirely in the Supreme Court, when I was a police guard cum court orderly, sitting in on a vast number of contested divorces.

The murky tales told by both sides and the evidence given by private detectives, who largely broke down doors, climbed into open windows and took photos of copulating couples (which I noted were carefully stared at by the court officials after being handed up to the judge, who no doubt had seen it all before) were accompanied by an audio recording made by the detectives, who seemed to enjoy their roles of impersonations which were sprinkled with lots of 'Oh Gods' until the judge told them to be silent.

It was a new world to me and Monday till Thursday I concluded that Adelaide the supposed city of churches had some grubbiness underneath, just like Wally Budd said. Adding to my amusement were the judges with their wigs and red robes guzzling jug after jug of water, though it was rumoured that many of the jugs held pure Gilbeys gin. Numbered amongst the QCs who thundered from the bar table was an eloquent gent who was by 2 p.m. half-sloshed after a long lunch. Richard III and Henry V were quoted in exchanges with the judge, whose nose was quite red. The QC's speech ran out by 4 p.m., when he fell back in his chair and went to sleep. The judge stumbled out to his chambers and I sat there until told by an official to go.

In contrast, Friday's advocate had a boring voice which droned on all day. I went to sleep and woke up to the sound of a floor polisher operated by an Italian lady who shook me back into the world. It was 6 p.m. and I sweated all weekend expecting an inspector to call but nothing happened.

Night shift came on Saturday at 11 p.m. and I was there bright-eyed and ready to take on the world. I was detailed a beat in Rundle Street where patrons flooded out from the theatres which were closing and crowds gathered waiting for the trolley buses (like the ones I used to repair) and which took them either to the west or the east of the city. They were happy crowds and a sense of euphoria came over me when I realised I was their protector. I was, at that point, in my own movie. Just like King Arthur in Camelot with his subjects. The street lights were soon dimmed, as this was a sleepy city. But crooks loved the dark. A fellow ran through the crowd bumping into the citizens and jumping up, touching the neon lights. I wished I was a blue ghost at this point because every eye turned round and stared at me as if I was Solomon, who could cut the baby in half. He was no baby and I had no sword. I thought about the law and disorderly behaviour, which was a substantial breach of decorum. Barrington v Austin was the judgement. I stiffened my tendons just like the drunken QC when he quoted *Henry V* and I acted. I placed my hand on his shoulder and said, 'You're nicked.' My first arrest. I did not caution him because I forgot the lines. Like a silent chook waiting to be fed, he walked along with me towards the gloomy city watch house.

GE had not come under my radar beam at that time. It took at least fifteen years for an appearance by the guide and I sometimes think, my god, what did he think of me in all those years? Where was he when I needed someone to talk to about my first arrest?

We stopped at a police call box to ring in and in that moment I felt a blow from behind which thrust my head on the open box. My hat fell off and my ears were jammed. The phone cord came off in my hand when I wormed my head out of the box, inch by inch like a corkscrew being removed from a wine bottle. My angry eyes lit on a scrawled piece of large black writing at the back of the box which said, 'Sergeant Mitchell sucks.' I never met the sergeant but he had an enemy in the ranks of the police. Consequences for the disconnected phone cord were hovering around, so, with that thought foremost, I scratched around the large bins and there was the culprit crouched down. I put on my battered hat to cover my red ears and hauled him to his feet. I kicked him in the behind just for good measure and had him now in a strong grip. There were no handcuffs in those days except the monstrosities which came out with

HMS *Buffalo* in 1836, so no one carried them. It was the same with the old Webley and Scott .45 revolver which was too heavy. Most of us then were able to have a police permit. Later on I bought a World War I 9mm Luger which I had to sell once the new firearms came in, which were .380 Brownings, an also useless weapon.

I frogmarched him along the park and he needed a pee. We stopped near a giant fig tree and he relieved himself. I was actually aiding and abetting him to urinate in a public place, but all the public toilets closed at 11 p.m. Then off we went again with my man carrying the phone with the dangling cord.

He pressed the button and spoke. 'Hello, hello, coming in with an arrest for piddling in a public place.'

I thought of letting him go but how could I explain the phone and the hat and my ears? I grew to like him on the walk back. But I was the protector, so I charged him at the station.

The sergeant asked about the phone cord. I told him.

His reply was 'You idiot.'

I really wished I was a blue ghost at this point because my morale had taken a battering and there would have been no point in telling him about my essay.

In spite of my night shift, I had to wait around till 10 a.m. for the court. I yawned and nearly fell asleep again. Derek Wilson, the el supremo magistrate, surveyed his packed courtroom of fearful subjects. DW noted every blink of an eye and no one dared speak out of turn. This was a man who could hear a snake fart in Egypt. He heard the facts from the prosecutor after I had given my evidence.

'Why didn't you charge him with assault, constable?'

I stood straight and put on my honesty face. 'Because I kicked him in the behind first, Your Honour.'

A slight smirk washed over his lips.

The man was fined and he was required to pay for the phone. I did not claim the hat because it made me look like a veteran, so I thought.

I had to get smarter and dreamed that night of Sergeant Mitchell and whatever he sucked. Maybe an ice cream (surely not the other). However, I did not make any enquiries – too much information, I guessed.

The shift changed to day shift and in the week leading up to Christmas

I was detailed on traffic point duty at a major city intersection. Friendly motorists would sometimes pass over small gifts – at times, a stocking or two – to the grateful permanent traffic men who were well known in the area.

A gent in a Jaguar with a tweed hat and a plummy voice handed me a brown bag tied with a red cord.

'Thank you,' I said in my best bedside voice while the car crept away with the driver waving out the window. I noted his car number and resolved to send him a Christmas card.

Later, I returned to base after the permanent traffic guy took over. I opened the bag in expectation of something good, which was dented when the smell came into my nostrils, because I had been left a bag of dog poo. I wrapped it up and put it in the bin.

An older cop who was usually loaded on most days with freebies in his Gladstone bag, no doubt from many grateful motorists, posed a question. 'Get anything for Christmas, young Ray?'

I pointed to the bin and he spotted the bag of dog poo.

'It was my turn.' He fell on the dinner table and laughed with tears running down his face. I had made his day. Whenever he spotted me, he would point and start into laughter again and I must say so did I.

But I knew I would get even. What goes around sometimes comes around. When I spotted the same Jaguar parked illegally in Rundle Street, I wrote out a sticker and placed it under the windscreen wiper and just waited nearby. The gent came into view and spotted the flapping sticker and raced towards the car. He snatched it off and looked around and spotted me. His tweed hat was askew and it was obvious he did not recognise me. His eyes bore an enraged look. 'Fair go, mate,' he yelled.

I looked him in the eye and watched him stew and blink. I did not blink. 'Have a good day and take your dog for a walk.'

He opened and closed his mouth in recognition. I am sure the bag was meant for one of the senior blokes but I happened to be there so I copped it. A rather expensive gift, I thought, and the inner man within me combined with the outer and laughed in unison. There was to be no more skulking around like a blue ghost and from then on my arrest record grew.

32

Jobs For the Boys

The term 'jobs for the boys' was hatched well before my time and I suspect it was originally intended for those fortunate few who were earmarked for advancement by the senior staff. It grew horns and the throw-away line marked many areas in the police department. Not many left the job because it was more of a calling, a form of womb to tomb, because there were jobs for the magpies and the fishes.

Most of the day, the fish men drank endless cups of tea, sometimes laced with a good spirit which also caused frequent dashes to the toilet where they sat and read the dog-eared *Playboy* magazines. Some of those men who were viewed as misfits by virtue of their conduct or personality were consigned to places for life. However, a variety of postings were attractive to people with agendas outside the framework of the police.

One of those jobs was called the Goldfish Bowl (cops are masters at giving a handle which is the butt of many jokes; speed cops are very good at it). The successful people who made it to the top floor were gathered in the twin towers of Angas Street and they were able to gaze down on the glassed enclosure containing the goldfish constables who had fallen through the cracks and were assigned to the detailing of vehicle keys. Yet that assignment had its good points, as far as the so-called internees thought, for they had power over who would get keys and which vehicle would be assigned. Most of those men were grumpy and moaned about everyone in the job but it paid to stay sweet with them because you could end up with a flat tyre in the boot and no wrench and it would be impossible to identify who was the culprit.

Finally the bosses who had some sense worked it out and started giving out on occasions a box of chocolates or a packet of cigarettes.

And all of them smoked so much that the Commissioner had to have NO SMOKING INSIDE signs put up. No worries, they went and filled up the cars' interiors with smoke and detailed a miserable boss a smoke-filled car with the keys. It was fun just to watch them say, 'Sorry, that is all we have got…sir.' I wondered then who was really in charge of the Goldfish Bowl.

Another place was the quaint French-style building called the Torrens Lake police station, just off the lawns near the lake. The member there was said to be usually engaged in shooing off the swans gathered on the banks where couples stretched out, but the cop on duty gathered intelligence about the dark shapes that prowled around, some of them prone on the grass when it was dark. I am confident that the expression cop-u-later had its roots from the Torrens Lake police station. To be objective, many of the duty men passed on into the CIB with reams of names stuck in their notebooks which were used to solve serious crimes, once the advent of some vicious murders became a feature in the landscape.

The Government House guard room at the intersection of King William Street and North Terrace is sited at the gate entrance just behind the Boer War memorial. On-duty cops rotated in three shifts over twenty-four hours and the staff were a mixed bag. For instance, one of them was a lover of Shakespeare and a millionaire, on paper; his many houses required him to spend most of the day checking his papers and on the phone, regarding his rental business. There was a World War II Desert Rat veteran with rows of ribbons who made and sold dolls annually at the Adelaide Royal Show. Visitors bought many dolls: they were careful not to sit on the pins and the wool spread across the desk in his operations. He also drank the best Scotch whisky with the head butler during night shift. Dimple brand, I am told.

Then there was Brian, who loved to entertain the Japanese tourists who took massive numbers of photos of the giant gates, which were usually closed. Brian would rush out to the gates when he heard clicking noises and just like an excited puppy would climb up the gates and scratch himself like a monkey, picking imaginary fleas and eating them as well. His antics might have fooled Jane Goodall. However, a senior officer with the personality of a concrete block was watching, and preparing a case for Brian to be admitted to the Adelaide Clinic at Gilberton. Funny about that, because later on the same officer spent many months in the clinic on a program of rehabilitation. An extensive report was about to be submitted about Brian's mental state when fortune rushed in and saved him.

He was on a boring night shift when he heard a lot of hollering from the big house and spotted steam vapours pouring out of the chimney. The old boilers had seen better days, as had the old boilers on the staff. Our valiant cop charged in and turned on all the taps, which released the pressure, and the day was saved. The Governor (naturally a British officer, which rankled with the population, sick and tired of appointments from thousands of miles away) wrote a glowing report about Brian and from that day on he was a protected bird. People laughed at him and said he was a clown yet he was always engaged in doing good works and kind deeds: he received many letters from the public. He was a religious man, but not an evangelist running around the suburbs, disturbing people and blaming Satan for all of the misery of their lives. He died later and I imagine him swinging on the pearly gates.

Many years ago, after he found out my address, he would bang on our front door on Sunday mornings and yell out, 'Up, up, Ray. Cup of tea milk and two sugars.'

My wife and I tolerated it for a while before we started to grumble.

We had slept in when once again the knocking started and my wife said, in a weary voice, 'Who the bloody hell is that?'

Kerry the four-year-old beat me to the door and opened it and said in her child's voice, 'It's bloody Brian.'

He never came again on a Sunday morning. I owe you an apology, Brian.

There was Mal the laconic recalcitrant Aussie bloke who hated pomp and ceremony, especially in the form of the brigadier who was the Governor's secretary. The brigadier had an annoying habit of going in and out of the gates wearing his bowler hat and waiting for salutes. He emerged early one morning in his best Italian suit and bowler hat with a brolly, and stood near Mal the republican outside the gates.

'Gidday, mate,' said Mal, which enraged the officer.

'Do you know who I am?'

To which Mal replied in his casual voice, 'No, but if you check with the office girls, I'm sure they'll tell you.'

The officer had nowhere near the intelligence of Mal and was stuck for words and rushed in to use the guard house phone, which was very busy with the millionaire checking his clients.

G put his hand over the phone and said, 'Yes?', unhappy that the pompous man had interrupted him.

The officer ran away again, determined to wreak revenge. Many minutes later, he came out in full uniform but Mal had made himself scarce in the toilet and G, the phone man, was busy typing an accident report from a member of the public. The bemedalled man marched along King William Street heading for the men in the twin towers.

All the cops were aware, because Mal rushed up and told them. The traffic men ducked into doorways as he passed and big Ron the thirty-year traffic man took off his hat and made a sweeping gesture and said in a loud voice which amused the passing crowd, 'Good morning, your majesty.'

An old rascal (the man with the bear suit) put his hat on back to front and when the brigadier turned around he was saluted just like Benny Hill. He made a complaint, which Mal answered by referring to the para which said, 'Staff members will not be saluted unless a uniform is worn.' Mal had won. The pompous man was transferred, no doubt pondering about Aussies and their humour. A civilian later replaced him.

Jury Guard

We clamoured for a turn of duty as guards because it was a live-in arrangement during murder trials, with three constables and a sergeant (intended to keep us in check but he out-drank the lot of us – including the all-male jury) assigned the details.

I watched the drama after a guilty verdict with the black cap placed upon the judge's head and sentence pronounced. It was commuted to a life sentence, which turned out to be about fifteen years. I was on duty in the Holden Hill police station in 1973. The office was packed but I recognised one man hanging back (sorry about the pun). I knew it was the man convicted when I was a guard. We read official papers that he was to report as part of a bail condition. I opened the journal and wrote down his full name and the reason why he reported.

He was amazed and queried how I knew him.

'I was a jury guard when you were sentenced.'

He shrugged and walked away and I never saw him again.

*

There were other lurks which topped up the low salary of a cop (often referred to as guaranteed poverty). Mostly they involved being in a clan with other moonlighters who were very good at it, including some future bosses. Even though it was illegal, a blind eye was turned unless a member of the public made a complaint. I washed cars for a hire car company. I picked cherries in the hills. I was a totaliser guard and did security at weddings. One wedding was high society and I guess I am still in the surgeon's daughter's album. I carted bricks with my former brother-in-law Ralph Powell, who was a West Torrens league footballer. I built shade houses and propagated native plants for sale. I was in the Army Reserve and made some tax-free money with that organisation. My wife Marlene held some good jobs in the hospitality industry. And last but not least I used to work the night shift inside a major shopping centre. Later on a became a bailiff and served debt summons. It was honest money and rather benign.

The only objection from the twin towers was working in pubs, as many of our punters were there with their eyes and ears well and truly open. It was like the old dirty ditty of 'Everybody's doing it', but don't get caught – the Eleventh Commandment.

33

Silvio Belotti

Retired Senior Sergeant Silvio Belotti wrote a great book which he named *Saloon Bar Socrates*. Published by Peacock Publishers of Kent Town, SA, it is a collection of his wisdom brimming with wonderful sayings and I must confess I have used some of them in my writings with his blessing.

Silvio was forced into an invalid retirement because an infected man in the front office of his command, the Tea Tree Gully police station, sneezed into his face. He suffered that night when his body swelled with meningitis, which was a close-run thing which left him stone deaf and stuck in his virtual death experience (different to an NDE). It was a sad end to the career of a much-loved man who treated his staff like his own children. Females were revered and always called 'Cherub' (and even to this day a high-ranking female confesses to me that she still feels the protection afforded to her by Silvio). Males were called 'brother', regardless of rank. I have no doubt that some commissioned officers full of their own importance were happy to see his back as it sailed out of the door forever, because it took some figuring out how to handle the brilliant man whose IQ numbered amongst the best in the job.

I observed his humour in full sail many times and always suppressed a giggle. One example occurred in 1976 when I was a general police senior sergeant and he was the admin man at the Holden Hill police station. I stopped off for a break around 8 p.m. and watched Silvio with his card-playing mates in their delayed meal. No one dared to interfere in those games. A missing child report had come in beforehand. Silvio was right on to it and had organised the operation – after all, he had written the operation order about missing persons. The troops finally found the child in the family tool shed and all was well.

A freshly commissioned officer, who was a nice guy, was not aware of the outcome and rushed into the lunch room like a rabbit whose burrow had been buried. He chucked questions left and right while the game went on. The guys were laughing at their hands.

Silvio then chose to put the officer out of his misery and, without looking up, answered all the questions obliquely. The officer was exasperated until Silvio told him of the outcome.

'What can I do then?'

Belotti did not look up from the game but reached into his jacket and pulled out a few dollars. 'You can get me a pasty with sauce,' and then added, 'sir.'

The boss was about to reach for the note when he realised he had been had. He walked out with the laughter of the hairy old men ringing in his ears.

There were huge files called PCOs which would occasionally rise like Lazarus from the grave because someone in an office somewhere was too scared to get rid of the old well fingered ones which had no significance. People who received one of these files just recycled them back to the source with a 'Not Known' or some other comment and they would lie in wait until a new clerk in the Commissioner's office regurgitated them once again and the files went back and forth once again for some decades. Silvio received one of those files which was called 'What to do about road accidents', an old chestnut. All that was being done was the best, outside of road engineering. Silvio had a notion and chucked the great file into the old besser block incinerator, watching the blue flames while they shrank the blue cover. The new boss was horrified and watched the licking flames, no doubt wondering about his career going up in flames but Silvio tried to save the boss by remarking, 'Relax, boss – even incinerators need a feed.'

He learnt hypnotism just after his induction from Western Australia to the SA Police as a young cadet. The cadets entered at sixteen years of age and had to ride horses in the mounted division headed by the former Lt Colonel Jack Cowley, a legendary figure, mainly in his own movie, who was a sledger of young people and a bully as well. The old mounties were men of great skill in their horsemanship, as was the leader, but they were clannish. Jack did not like anyone in the job with an Italian name and made no secret of it, insisting as an excuse that he had fought against them in the war. Matters came to a head when Silvio was called into Jack's office and had to listen to the abuse.

'I don't want any Dagos in the job.'

Silvio knew his days were numbered. If Jack had bothered to check Silvio's file, he would have read that his parents fled the Blackshirts in the 1920–30 era. He would have read that Silvio was a drover when he was twelve years of age and rode like an Aussie, crouched over the saddle, not straight back like Jack's men.

Jack put Silvio on Rodney, his most favoured old horse, who loved Jack. Jack vowed to never speak to Silvio again and only spoke to Rodney. 'Rodney, bring the Dago here.'

And there was Silvio clinging to the mane, helpless to stop the sideways movement, while the old mounties fell down laughing.

Silvio hatched a plan with his hypnotism, which had been tried out successfully on his peers. He had one of the favoured sergeants doing tricks without him knowing about it. His peers loved the demonstrations. The time had come to execute the plan.

Jack pranced up and down the men assembled in three ranks, at the same time swishing his riding crop and berating people, to the amusement of the senior men, who really encouraged him.

The young master clicked his fingers and right on cue the favourite sergeant stepped out of the front rank and planted a kiss full on Jack's lips. Jack had a panic attack and struck the man on the face with the riding crop, and then ran back to the office to brood on how it had all happened, no doubt thinking his favourite was a homosexual – Jack would tell tales about what he did to such people in the war. But someone told Jack to call in Belotti. They had watched his demonstrations a few weeks ago.

Silvio stood silent a few moments later in Jack's office.

'Here's a one-way ticket back to WA. Don't let me see your beer-sodden countenance ever again.'

Silvio went straight to the police union, who also had enough of Jack and the many complaints he drew. Silvio was advised to cash in the ticket, which he did, and was transferred out of harm's way to another section.

Silvio has well and truly outlived Jack Cawley. I wonder at times what happened to Jack in the afterlife. After all, he wasn't a serial killer but a good family man by all accounts and a soldier who was just locked into the prejudices of the times. Maybe he has returned as an Italian restaurant owner. Who knows? It is not something I would ever ask GE.

34

Bugsy

The nickname seemed incongruous to me in consideration of his over six-foot strongly built frame. However, it was a handle which stuck to Brian Knowles like golden syrup to the fingers. Maybe the name drifted in after a one-liner cast towards him, after hearing one of his many impersonations back in his days at the Elizabeth CIB, where his career blossomed under the guidance of Detective Sergeant 'King' O'Malley and Laurie Draper, who became a police commissioner. Perhaps the nickname just referred to the US gangster Bugsy Siegel. I knew Brian then but I was acquainted with him when he went into uniform at Para Hills in the 70s at a time when Elizabeth was a hot bed of crime, mainly due to the socio-economic conditions when jobs were lost at GMH.

Elizabeth was either a path to a brilliant career or a trip to destruction and Brian fitted in well for the times until the waters were muddied, shaken and stirred with debris floating to the top, which led to depression, followed by a forced invalid retirement upon Brian, my friend and believer of all things beyond the veil, who shared with me his belief in guides and reincarnation. His wife Carol was a great believer as well.

The night of his last confrontation with an armed offender who was determined to kill a cop was a pivotal moment for Brian. A loaded double-barrel shotgun was the weapon of choice for the dangerous man, who was at his back fence with Brian on the other side. Brian engaged him in a dialogue while all the time the man was waving the gun to and fro and making threats. The five-foot fence was easy for the gunman, who maintained the weapon close to the head of my friend. Brian was dry in his throat and his voice was cracking after thirty minutes of speaking. He was in great peril and the crook knew it. All this time, Brian thought about Carol and the kids from two marriages each. He thought about the caravan trip they were soon to take and then the thought of Raymond his mentally challenged son came into his mind. What would Raymond do if he lost his father?

The .380 police weapon was inside a shoulder holster. It was underpowered and any sudden moves by Brian would result in his death. A migraine belted his head from front to the back and then the crook went silent and cocked the weapon. The sound on the humid night was like a cricketer striking a ball with a bat. Clunk.

Brian spoke again. 'Fire your gun and shoot me. A nice clean hole in the head, that's all.' It was a big risk but Brian could see it appealed to the sick man.

'No tricks. Just hand over your gun, butt first.'

Brian did and counted on the plan working because there were two safety catches on the weapon – the normal one and the butt had to be squeezed.

The crook leered and took the weapon and cocked it. He released the safety catch and said in a croaked voice, 'You're dead now, copper.' He squeezed the trigger.

The gun didn't work but Brian's plan did. The crook looked away for the moment and the next thing he knew was when he woke up in hospital with a broken jaw. Brian had punched him senseless. Brian received an honourable mention, which was well below what he ought to have got, such as a bravery medal. Nothing would stem the flow of his nightmares after that episode.

Years later while he was riding a desk and not accepted for any further promotion, a complaint was made about Brian trying to sell AMP insurance policies and making threats that if people didn't buy one they would be stuck in an office. He was also under investigation for an array of lollies and condom machines which he owned. We were aware of his activities but no one complained. Indeed, I bought one of the policies, which didn't pay too well later, but that is life.

There are times in our lives when much can oppress us. Maybe it is a giant dose of self-evaluation, opinions of others either warranted or unfounded. Perhaps the general misery of loved ones closes in on us. A misery breeds its own company. It sticks to us like an insect which crawls in our ears in the night.

The factors built up in Brian's mind and did not help in his efforts to beat the black dog of depression. Great sorrow descended on him with protracted periods that could have been released with therapy but it was not offered to him. He reached a point when there was nothing left in his vacant space to grieve on. No more mantras to God. Nobody came. It was a turning point for him because it caused a recharge of his batteries. He started his engine. He engaged the gears, let in the clutch and just steered away into a new world of hopeful expectations and all done by Brian himself.

However, a shadow remained silently smirking inside of him and it grew like an asparagus patch not thinned out. The pills, potions and creams helped a little but did not stop the bitterness of the flashbacks. He was painted into a corner and embroiled into a world of a lot more unfounded assumptions. He had, of course, resigned well and truly by then and planned the great trip. They took it. It became Carol's nightmare.

Brian died aged 64 years while on the caravan trip to Darwin. She was left with the mess of bringing back his body (packed in ice) a week later. I attended the funeral of my friend. A good cop, a good detective. A good husband and father. An obsessive moonlighter – though I whispered to my friend in the night after I saw some of the bosses who were worse moonlighters than Brian. 'Everybody's doing it, mate.' Before the night came, we spoke about his mother-in-law's rocking chair which kept rocking long after her death, until a priest was called. We were on the same plane.

Me: GE, I am in grief about my mate but I felt helpless.

GE: You did your best. There was nothing you could do.

Me: But the department could have given him some therapy.

GE: How do you know they didn't? People do not share everything, you know.

There is always wisdom in his words and I thought no more on it.

35

Fear and Hatred

I slipped back in time reviewing all the incidents which I had forgotten about. A thought sprang into my brain with two words, 'fear' and 'hatred'. I knew how fear graduates into hatred which can boil over into violence. A few stories came to light, so I quickly sharpened the pencil and spoke once again to GE, re-visiting stuff from 1958 to 1988.

Me: GE, do you remember 1958 when the woman stabbed her partner in the chest with a machete and Brian yanked the blade out of his chest while he lay on the footpath till the plain clothes guys came along and arrested her?

GE: I forget nothing. It is just like yesterday and I felt your horror when you thought Brian had killed him.

Me: Funny, though, the man went back to live with her afterwards.

(He did not reply about the actions of the man after the case was reduced to unlawful wounding.)

Me: I am moving on to 1972 at Holden Hill when Ken K and I discovered a case of incest by a father with his daughters. I was horrified about it.

GE: It has been going on for years but it was not on with my tribe. A warrior once succumbed to the overtures of his daughter and he was executed with a blow to the head after the elders pronounced punishment.

Me: Behind my street in1973. The Greens. The brother stabbed in the throat by his mad sister with a piece of glass. I rode in the back of the ambulance in case he made a dying declaration. I had to hold his head still at the RAH when the doctor removed the slivers.

GE: You were not too keen on that, were you?

I moved on to 1988 without any reply.

Me: The terrible scene of the triple murder and suicide at Windsor Gardens when I had to guard the bodies until the detectives came. It has stayed in my memory every since. It was a case which had hardly any publicity.

GE: Madness ruled that night.

Me: Thank you once again for listening.

GE: I see your computer skills are coming along.

Me: Could I send a message to you by computer?

I heard the sound of a shuddering gasp by my left ear where he chooses to stand. The gasp which he is prone to at times is just like an exasperated school teacher when the class doesn't get it right.

GE: Spare me. I have more to do than tap at keys. Goodnight, Raymond. Write to me when the book is finished. I have to attend a meeting with the big boss. No, not going back into human life. Had enough of that. I could see your ears pick up about that. That's it. God bless!

I went on with some more persistent questions which he apparently knew all about anyway, and I reflected on that.

36

Devitt's Paddock

Devitt's paddock was once open land called savannah light forest which had seen the marks of footprints for thousands of year on its grassy bed. The Kaurna tribe used it as a route to the Adelaide Hills during the warmer weather when the game was varied and plentiful. They would pull down their (surprisingly waterproof) wurlies made of branches and leaves and move on, leaving no trace of their journeys. It was an area which had watched over the chiefs and the clans, smiling benevolently on them, and never concerned about the colour and customs of the humans. All that the area asked for was no destruction of its flora but sadly since 1836 when white men came to the shores the under-storey became extinct within a few short years. Some of the giant red gums survived the cross-cut saws due to the urgings of a pocket of enlightened citizens who fiercely resisted any further destruction but they were a handful, up against people with grand plans.

The area had shrunk by the time of the Devitt family, who owned the dairy and adjoining land where all of the dairy herds and other animals grazed. The drums of war sounded in 1939 and the cutting down of giant trees halted. The citizens were called upon to support the war against the Axis; however, the paddock remained neutral because the former tribes had battled against others and blood had flowed into the red clay.

It was a great playground of many acres, with trees to climb, bats to spot, magpies to contend with, and possums with their bright eyes shared tree hollows with a vast array of colourful parrots. Dave and Morrie, my friends in the street, made full use of the land on weekends and summer nights.

War in its unstoppable fashion caused great changes to the people of this country. As kids we wore green plastic discs around our necks with our name, blood groups and so on. My blood group was B positive. Dad dug a bomb shelter but it all fell in due to heavy rain.

A company of US engineers camped opposite with their forage caps and fancy overcoats. And the inevitable chewing gum. Women cadged smokes off them, some left when they left, and we missed the men, who were really only boys. We missed their colour and their laughter and their kindness to us kids. They packed up their gear one night and not a trace could be seen of them ever having lived in the paddock. The sirens stopped after the threat of invasion dissipated. Our damaged young men, crippled in mind, body and spirit, came home in dribs and drabs and we heard stories of some of them being carted away by men wearing white coats, never to be seen again.

But the one constant still sat there unmoved, waiting as it always had for more groups of humans. The Italians escaping from the Blackshirts in the 1930 period. Eighty years before saw Pastor Kavel escaping from Germany because of religious persecution, walking from Klemzig (to the west of the paddock) and settling in the Barossa Valley, where wonderful wine was produced. Some of the Italians and the third generation Germans lived nearby for a time, until internment reared its ugly head.

There were too many memories which I had buried. An enquiry had to be made: I never ventured to the paddock after Mum sold out and lived with us in Modbury in 1974 years later in 1986 and I was the only senior sergeant available. I drove to the house, took some notes and later sat near the remnants of the paddock soaking up some atmosphere and memories. A police radio crackled out a message about a motorcycle accident. This took me back to 1954 when I owned an Indian Pony Scout motorcycle and sidecar and came to grief against a wall on a main road. I touched the scar on my right cheek under the eye where thirteen stitches were dug in without anaesthetic. Dad stashed the bike away and I never rode it again.

My eyes misted over when I saw the stumps of the great red gums cut down by an owner who feared branches might fall. I thought about the new kids on the block who would never have their own personal acres to play on, with their imagination running wild.

I was about to turn the radio up a notch when I heard a plane in the sky. And another flashback came in with the sound of piston engines spluttering with the props occasionally pausing and I remembered the victory flight by the old Lancaster (G For George) with the crew hanging out of the doors and windows and waving to the kids. It was so low that it blew our hair about as we waved back at our heroes. Each kid thought the crew was waving to them and some imagined that they called out the names of the kids. I could not wait to tell Dad, who had finished his night shift and cycled back on his old bike with the kerosene lamp. He cycled the twenty miles to and from Findon each day without complaint.

I thought about heroes and then uttered something out loud. 'You were my hero, Dad, you really were.'

I thought about GE and he deserved a bit of credit as well. 'Yes, GE, if you are there, you are also my hero.'

I drove away and circled the block one last time and saw the changes in the street. Duplexes and courtyard houses had replaced the giant blocks and the bull-nosed verandas. Gardens once loaded with every fruit imaginable were no more; instead, families sat in their homes watching endless television programs with ridiculous plots, or sat outside on a cramped patio all with the street noise of screeching car tyres and violent husbands shouting and cursing.

There are street humps there now, which prevent cars being raced abreast by the clowns who do not care about the kamikaze old folk with their wheel frames blindly crossing the road. Most of the other, much saner drivers have mobile phones so far in their ears that the devices would show up on an X-ray. They might be thinking about tomorrow, rather than the moment, and this is what people call progress.

A boy ran down the street bouncing a football. He was wearing a red and blue jumper and it signalled my time in the school team when I came out from under a pack, dazed, and ran towards the goals. I kicked the football straight through the two posts and shot my arm up in the air in excitement, till the coach yelled out, 'Congratulations. You just kicked a goal for the other side. Ours is that way.' He pointed that way and I shrank.

I remember the learn to swim campaign when I was eleven when a great lout jumped in the pool on my back and there I was swallowing water. My breath stopped just before the OBE started and finally I was pulled out, wondering what all the fuss was about. I did not see lights on that occasion.

The night was still, yet the stars were not as bright and I thought one word: pollution. All I heard on this still night was the sound of traffic, which was never loud years ago. In those days, the sounds of the lions roaring at the zoo some ten miles away could be heard when they enjoyed their nightly feed. No chance of hearing that nowadays.

At the end of the war I had a job with the local mobile greengrocer distributing the produce and derby collecting the next day – the youngest bailiff in the street. My first pocket money I saved to buy Mum a mirror which she treasured all of her life.

The tramways as mentioned had a dark side, a dark side of voyeurism. The fence bordered on the parklands and holes were bashed in the fence to watch the copulating couples in cars during their lunch breaks. I peered out once and saw a priest with his white collar humping away at a parishioner. I know it was one of his flock because the older apprentice went to his church. Hypocrisy once again and my innocence was quickly fading.

But what a learning curve that place was. I was 16 years of age and tested in all the vehicles at the tramways. I drove a tram, a bus, a double decker, a trolley bus and a great GMH army vehicle and passed all the tests. I doubt if kids would get that chance in today's world.

On my return journey along Portrush Road, I remember walking home with groups of kids after we had watched the midnight horror session and being scared out of our wits with the images of Boris Karloff with the overhanging eyebrows and educated voice opening a great door and speaking with a threat. 'What lies behind the green door, master?'

We all imitated him on the walk home until the local cop rode up on his bike and told us to be quiet because we were keeping the good people awake with our laughter.

At home that night, I started a session with GE again.

Me: I guess you know where I have been, GE?

GE: Yes. I told you that you had to face it, didn't I?

Me: Right once again. It brought back memories. I'm sad for the kids who live there now.

GE: You are only remembering the good stuff. Think about it.

Me: Yes. The kids that died of many diseases. The lack of vitamins and food slopped in gravy and fat. Helped to kill my dad, you know.

GE: It is a better time for you. The population is not hung up and wearing ties and so on.

Me: You got that right, GE, in your brief manner. Not wearing a tie. It tells it all. But I wouldn't have missed it for quids.

GE: You had to be born in that time.

Me: Largely we have become a generation spoiled with access to everything. Goods, abundance, and we fear to leave our comfort zones.

GE: It won't be like that forever, Raymond. (Which reminded me how much he knows about the future and climate change.)

I drove back to the base and submitted my report.

The Next Day

'How did it go last night, sergeant?

'Tough stuff. Christ, there seem to be a lot of perverts around lately, porn and all that stuff. Did you see much of it in your day?'

'It was always there but not porn. Just old flashers really.'

The air was expectant and Jim was probing, so I broke into his thoughts. 'There was an old bugger called Bill when I grew up in South Payneham.'

'I heard you took on a job at Devitt Avenue.'

'Yep, I grew up there. We had a giant acreage right opposite as well as one-acre house blocks in the street.'

'It vaguely rings a bell.'

'Yes, sadly it has all changed. All the great trees were chopped down. Got a minute? I'll tell you something, OK?'

Jim nodded.

'Old Bill lived near with his mother, I heard. She would be as ancient as the old trees. He would hide in amongst the four-foot marshmallow weeds and dart out when he saw kids coming. He stumbled about at times like a beetle with the gout and was barely head and shoulders above the weeds. Sun, rain, hail, he was always dressed in the same old fashion with his old white short-sleeved shirt displaying his red skin and wide brown shorts with his skinny red legs staring out like asparagus shoots.

'The shorts were permanently stained with bodily excretions. The bulge in the front showed the most favoured part of his body. God had blessed him with a huge purple-headed varmint which peered around under the shorts. It seemed to be waiting like a cobra for an unsuspecting victim. My mates were onto him with his flashing habits because no sooner was he in someone's space than he would fumble around exposed until his eyes glazed over. It got to be serious because he searched around for a child who would explore up his shorts.'

'Bloody hell,' said Jim.

'When not in company with Joe Heading, the local cop who detained him every time he saw him in the paddock, he could be seen skulking around schools, leering over the fence looking for fresh meat. There were great weals on his face where fathers had punched him. Hair was missing in clumps probably pulled out by his mother. My granddad took to him once and knocked him out cold and he lay in the grass all night. My dad, dry as usual, said to me, "Never had toys to play with." However, we never heard of a child being raped and his disgusting style was confined to flashing. Sad, really, isn't it? He vanished for a few months into gaol and then returned. I saw him skulking around in the street where a new girl had moved in. Don, a friend, watched when he placed a note in the hedge. We waited and retrieved it. Don read the note out loud: "Meet me after school in the half built houses and I will show you my tool and give you a ten-shilling note." We made a decision and took the note with us when we banged on the door.

'A grey-haired lady opened the door and said in a gruff tone, "What do you want?"

'Don thrust the note into her hand and she read it.

'"Where did you find this, boy?"

'Don pointed at the hedge. "Old Bill the perv put it in the hedge. We thought you would like to know."

'She flashed her nicotine-stained teeth and the smell of liquor came out. She told us to wait and then brought out a tray full of fresh lamingtons, which we gobbled up with glee and then left with bits of coconuts all over us. We felt good because we had saved the girl from the clutches of Old Bill.

'Two detectives hid behind the hedge later in the day and waited for the girl. She walked to the houses where old Bill waited in his shorts. Just as he dropped his shorts and the varmint appeared, the cops rushed in and hauled him out. The last I saw of Old Bill was when he was thrown into the sidecar with his little red legs hanging over the side and a great red-faced detective was sitting on him when they drove away.'

'Did time, I suppose, Ray?'

'I imagine, Jim. Anyway, Joe Heading spoke to Dad about it all and told them what a good job we had done.'

'"Good job, son," said Dad. "Bill won't be around for many years."

'Mum was happy, as were the rest of the mothers in the street, except Dave's, who had died a long time ago, but his older sisters were happy.'

'Shit,' said Jim. 'Anything else, sarge?'

I gathered my thoughts and went on, as I had by now found an expanded audience of more cops.

'Some of us joined the 1st Maylands Scouts group. Dave and others thought they were too old for the scouts and trained at Chamberlains gym on Wellington Road. I love to tie knots and soon passed the tenderfoot exams. My favourite knot was the bowline, which I never forgot and used later when I was on the cliff rescue squad and abseiling.'

Tom interrupted me. 'The forerunner of the Star Force.'

I went on, 'There was something about the leader of the Scouts which disturbed me. My ears pricked up whenever he strolled about but I kept mum. We were on camp at Golden Grove on a farm and in the milking shed where we were to sleep during the night when I heard the leader prowling about and felt blankets being pulled off and saw flickering torchlights inside the shed. The next day we were lined up and told to strip. We were shy boys then and covered our groins with our hands when he played a fire hose over all of us. His eyes fixated on our groins and on our bums as well when he went behind with the hose and the freezing cold water.

'He gave us towels to dry ourselves and most of us walked home, which was a long way off. I told Dad and he was furious and let Joe Heading know. It all came out when one of the kids confessed to his dad that he had been sodomised. The leader went to gaol later on and Dad stopped my attendance at the Scouts. The sweet world of innocence was coming adrift. And I knew it.'

'Bloody hell, Ray – my son is in the Scouts.'

'Don't panic, John. That was years ago and screening has got rid of the suspects. But keep an eye on him during Scout camps.'

'You bloody betcha.'

We were due for a rehearsal at a funeral at Berry's on Magill Road for a well liked high-ranking boss. I drew out a car later and picked up some of the troops for the detail. Joe asked me on the way to repeat the story and added, 'Crikey, you have had an interesting life, sarge.' I did not tell him how interesting and that I had a guide called GE who had watched over me and protected me, for God knows what, and was still in my life. I concluded with a few more words but was not ready to tell him about GE and my writings.

'During the war there was a company of US soldiers camped in Devitt's paddock and as well there were Gypsies.'

'Gypsies. Didn't know we had any anywhere or about the Yanks.'

'Mum's younger sister started hanging around them until she was chastised by Mum. "Going off to see the soldiers, I see, with your cheap musk perfume, your ankle straps, your rouge as well. Mind how you go, girl."'

'Ankle straps?' Joe grinned.

'True, mate, true.'

We turned into the driveway of the funeral home where my parents had been buried and the old memories came back. I shut them out as quickly as I could – I needed no distractions because the formal occasion coming up was to be executed with precision. It was all over and we drove back to the base.

'A quiet moment, sarge.'

'Yes, Joe, too many funerals. I sensed Dad about. His Lifebuoy soap smell lingered on him. He was buried here in 1974, and Mum in 1985.'

Silence dominated the remainder of the short journey, with both of us deep in our own personal world.

Five years later I was out of the police and working in the sheriff's office at Elizabeth in the northern suburbs of Adelaide. The communications with GE came on in a rush, usually on weekends, as did tarot readings for many workmates. I was advised in my writings that I had made the choice to retire from the police at age fifty-five years in spite of great increases in the salaries of the police. Sadly, almost bimonthly, I attended funerals of my former police colleagues, which says something about the combined effects of stress in the job. No amount of money can free the accumulated stress which has built over thirty years.

37

GE and Me

This book's title entered my right front lobe when I considered the ramifications of writing a story such as this – an autobiography of a life which contained strange feelings of abandonment, though I had no reason to experience such an emotion due to my loving adoptive parents. Sure, times were tough for most of the citizens but I found out, once I was embroiled with migrants entering the country, what trials and tribulations they went through, so any thoughts of 'why me' were soon off the screen of life. On another note about abandonment, studies have revealed that a child of tender years can feel those surges, so somewhere along the line our DNA must hold it in, locked away in our shadow selves.

Then along came the OBEs and sicknesses bounced back like a rubber ball and I never knew that GE was standing nearby not revealing himself, maybe wanting to screech out loud, 'No, don't do that, Raymond.' Then came the time when I was ready, in the middle age of my life. The title set me up for a barrage of ridicule. Cops and other folk in similar professions are not expected to walk around talking to (or writing and expecting answers from) a Red Indian guide. From my experience during my careers, one could quickly became a figure of fun. So what? I don't care now. Age causes that.

I sat in the rumpus room in my computer chair with pad and pen and within few seconds of deep breathing some surprising dialogue emerged.

GE: Yes, there will be questions of credibility but you are beyond rejection now.

Me: You're right as usual. I have something to say, though, which I never did, and it came out in a dream a few nights ago when we were once again sitting by the lake and tossing pebbles in it. You were smiling and it seemed to me that you or some energy had put me in my middle age with like-minded folk who also had a secret spiritual life and who maybe spoke to a muse or someone. I know a writer who speaks to her muse. She is a great writer.

GE: That would be Sharon Kernot. Finally, at last you have got it. Yes, it came along when you were ready. Brian, Silvio, Todd and others.

Me: You, or maybe the angel Gabriel, put me with Ann to keep me grounded. To keep the ego in check, I reckon.

GE: Right. All part of the plan, and do not forget your two kids, whose take on this life has finally shown up, but they had a time when they walked away from it as well.

Me: That much I know.

GE: Stay writing. It keeps the brain cells going and the brain controls much of the body. Once it shuts down, so do the rest of the bodily functions. I can't say at this stage what will be published because so many factors affect the predictions, though this book, being a first-hand account, is a bit different to many others of the same genre. They all seem to be hung up with a lot of narrative and all have been written before, many times.

Me: Your help has been astounding. Thank you again.

GE: Good, Raymond. God bless till we meet again.

Me: But not for a while, GE, I hope – too much to do.

I put my pen down and opened the manila folder which was bulging with old yellowing paper with some words scratched out and some spillages of wine. A piece of garlic was stuck inside the cover and its odour rose up to greet me. I also took the sunflower seeds which had sprouted a few days ago from inside the folder (seeds which I use to feed parrots in the garden) and put them in a jar. I will plant them soon and they will remind me, over and over, of the fun which GE and I had together.

Fun aside, I wonder why I was chosen to be protected from physical harm all my life when other comrades bore the scars on dangerous encounters. There must have been a giant hand plucking away leaving me high and dry. Maybe it is just that God works in mysterious ways.

Eskimo saying: Yesterday is ashes, tomorrow is wood. Only today does the fire burn bright.

www.ingramcontent.com/pod-product-compliance
Lightning Source LLC
Chambersburg PA
CBHW030907080526
44589CB00010B/194